DANNY BOY

PRESS
A Superior Publishing Company

P.O. Box 115 • Superior, WI 54880
(715) 394-9513 • www.savpress.com

DANNY BOY

Karen M. Collins
and
Family
and
Friends

Karen M. Collins

First Edition

First Printing

15 14 13 12 10 9 8 7 6 5 4 3 2 1

ISBN 13: 978-1-937706-00-5

Library of Congress Catalog Card Number: 2011946155

Published by:

Savage Press
P.O. Box 115
Superior, WI 54880

Phone: 715-394-9513

E-mail: mail@savpress.com

Web Site: www.savpress.com

Printed in the U.S.A.

INTRODUCTION

On the day after Thanksgiving in November of 1984, Dan had an operation for rectal cancer. He was given a 50% chance of living more than 5 years.

On the day after Thanksgiving in November of 2010, Dan started his first chemo treatment for Stage 4 lung cancer.

On the day after Thanksgiving in November of 2011, Dan was buried. The Precious Lord carried him home on November 22.

DEDICATION

Danny Boy is dedicated to my husband, Daniel E. Collins, an Irish lad at heart, and a loving man who demonstrated his belief and trust in God the Father, the Son, and the Holy Spirit.

At the moment of his death, Dan reached his hand up to the Precious Lord who carried him into life everlasting.

MY STORY

Welcome to our CaringBridge website. We've created it to keep friends and family updated about our loved one. Get started by reading the introduction to our website, My Story.

Visit often to read the latest journal entries, visit the photo gallery, and write us a note in our guestbook.

Background Story

Today we learned that Dan has Stage-4 advanced lung cancer, which has metastasized (spread) to both lungs and to his lymph system. He will begin chemotherapy on the day after Thanksgiving. He will have chemotherapy weekly for about six months. Radiation may also be used. A PET scan, a CT scan of his brain, and a CT scan of his throat and neck will also be done before starting the chemotherapy.

Meg Likar Lontz, Dan's niece, suggested that we start a caring bridge site so that all our family and friends can keep updated with his progress. We used the caring bridge for a friend and co-worker the past few months and thought it was a wonderful site so I will do my best to keep it updated.

On October 9th, Dan started having shortness of breath, followed by a deep cough, and then he lost his voice on November 3rd. He was prescribed oxygen at night and a nebulizer five times a day and his condition did not improve.

After several tests and a biopsy, we were shocked to learn that he had cancer and it was this far advanced.

Today our four children Dan, Pat, Joe and Mary Lou, joined us to meet with the Dr. Mihailo Lalich, a Hematology/Oncology specialist for two hours followed by an appointment with an ENT specialist, Kimberly Lakhan to look at his throat and vocal cords. It was a long, stressful day, with lots of tears by all.

Dan wants to fight this cancer. 26 years ago this week, we learned he had rectal cancer and he won that battle and he is now ready to fight this battle. We were told if he did not have Chemo, he would have 4-6 months to live. If he does have it, the average life with this stage cancer is 8-12 months or longer, God Willing. Our kids assured him that he will not be on this journey alone, they will all be at his side helping any way they can. Dan and I have been married for 49 wonderful years and it goes without saying, we will walk this road hand in hand as we do every day, and as we did 26 years ago.

Our immediate plans are to search for a rental, (a condo, twin home, or apartment) in Superior or Duluth starting in December so we will not have to deal with driving in the bad weather and snow removal. We will let everyone know our new address and phone when we find a place to live.

Your prayers are appreciated very much. We are blessed with wonderful children and grandchildren to help us during these coming months. We are also blessed with many friends and neighbors to support us. We appreciate all the emails and calls you have sent us these past weeks.

The Lord is with us and we know He will keep Dan in the palm of His hands during this time. We will also pray for strength to remember His presence in the days ahead.

JOURNAL ENTRIES

Monday, November 22, 2010 6:28 PM, CST

Tomorrow we head up to Superior to stay with Mary Lou and Don Griffith, Logan, Kalen, and Nate Collins, our children and grandchildren for the rest of the week. On Wednesday, Dan will receive a PET Scan of his whole body, a CT Scan of his throat, and a MRI of his brain. Mary Lou will be with us. It will be a long day for Dan starting at 9 and ending with the last scan at 2:30 PM. On Thursday, we will all head over to enjoy a Thanksgiving dinner in Duluth with our son, Pat, and Tambrey, and our grandchildren, Brennen and Reid. Dan wants to make the pumpkin pie so he will-he makes the crust from scratch and it always tastes wonderful. On Friday morning, we head back to SMDC for Dan's first chemotherapy.

So far we have found one two bedroom furnished condo in Duluth in Beacon Point. It is right of 21st and 35 and looks over Lake Superior. We will be looking at it tomorrow. Larry Bowman, a neighbor on the lake, and owner of Bowman Properties in Duluth graciously offered to search for other furnished condos for us. If he cannot find one, we will stay the month of December at Beacon Point and see how we like it.

We pray that all the scans being done tomorrow are free of cancer. However, Dr. Lalich assured us that if there is cancer in the brain, he has been very successful with radiation treatments. Dan and I appreciate all the wonderful comments on this site, the cards and calls. We are very blessed to have such wonderful friends and family walking this journey with us. Please pray for him again tomorrow. Thank you everyone.

Tuesday, November 23, 2010 7:44 AM, CST

When you walk through a storm, keep your head up high and don't be afraid of the dark. At the end of the storm, there's a golden sky and the sweet silver song of a lark. Walk on Walk on with hope in your heart and you will never walk alone. This song is going through my head this morning. The Lord is holding Dan in the palm of HIS hand this morning.

Tuesday, November 23, 2010 4:24 PM, CST

On December 1, we will be moving into a condo at the Beacon Pointe Resort in Duluth MN. You can type in their name and go to their website and look at the 2 bedroom condo. We are on second floor. It is very beautiful and they have a pool, hot tub and exercise room so we will enjoy that. We will see Lake Superior every day.

Our address will be: Beacon Pointe Resort, Condo #202, 2100 Water Street, Duluth, MN. We will have underground heated parking so that will be wonderful. It is all furnished—all we have to do is bring our clothes.

Tuesday, November 23, 2010 6:22 PM, CST

A neighborhood Angel appeared on Buskey Bay Drive this morning. I went out and shoveled enough snow so I could drive the Van down from our upper garage and pack it. After packing it, I went back in the house and we did not take off for a couple hours. When we came out to the car, the driveway was plowed, including the driveway for the upper garage. When I was in the house, I called

Cory Holsclaw and told him he did not need to come out to plow because I was able to get out. Now we hear from our neighbor, Barb that the lower driveway is all plowed and she also was plowed out. We have a suspicion that we know the angel, but not sure. Whoever you are, thank you from the bottom of our heart.

Wednesday, November 24, 2010 4:18 PM, CST

Busy day today. Dad started at SMDC at 9:00 this morning with lab work followed by a PET scan of the body and a CT scan of the throat. The radiologist spoke with us immediately after these scans were completed. The PET scan showed a few lymph nodes in the neck that are cancer. There was also one small spot in the colon that he believed was not very worrisome, as it was only one single spot and if was a problem should have many spots.

The CT of the throat showed the paralysis of the vocal cord but no tumor around the cords.

No other areas of the body showed any cancer other than the lungs that were known. After a break for lunch and Dad to use his nebulizer, he then had an MRI of his brain. Again the radiologist came out to let us know immediately that there was no spread of cancer to the brain.

All in all—very good news today. Mom and Dad tired after such a busy day, but it was definitely worth the good news that the cancer has not spread anywhere else.

Prayers are working. Keep them up.

Love, Mary Lou

Thursday, November 25, 2010 8:29 AM, CST

Dan and I wish all of you a Happy and Blessed Thanksgiving. We are both feeling very relieved this morning after our good news yesterday. Tomorrow morning starts the chemo. We plan to return to Iron River after Dan's treatment. Dan and Ann Collins, our kids from Appleton will arrive Saturday to spend time with us and to help us pack for our move to Duluth on December 1. Today we all enjoy Thanksgiving dinner in Duluth with the family.

Mary Lou was amazing yesterday. She has been in the Radiology Department at SMDC for over ten years and everywhere we went they were hugging her and treated us wonderful. Radiologists do not normally come out and talk to the family, or show them the scans and x-rays, but they did for us. We owe that to Mary Lou. The doctors and staff thanked us for her and how blessed they are that she is working with them. Even though it was a long day, especially for Dan, everyone made it as comfortable for us as possible. Dr. Lalich, our oncologist also called us last night to go over all the results. We are very thankful for all that. Thank you!

Friday, November 26, 2010 5:07 PM, CST

We had a great thanksgiving dinner yesterday in Duluth with our two families up there. Today our first day of chemotherapy went very well. Mary Lou drove us and stayed with this during it all. We were at the clinic about 3.5 hours. If you are on Facebook, you will see Dan sitting in a recliner looking out over Lake Superior. The staff was all very competent and friendly. The nurse has been there many years and she said that there are very little side effects with these meds when they are given once a week and they have been very effective. She also encouraged Dan to do as much exercising as he can during this treatment so he stays strong. She was happy to hear we have a treadmill and swimming pool at our new condo complex.

We are home in Iron River now for three days to pack. Our son Dan and his wife Ann are arriving tomorrow from Appleton to help. We will move in on Dec. 1 and Don Griffith, our son-in-law, and son Pat will meet us at the condo to help move things out of the car. Thanks for all those in Iron River who have offered to help us pack and move. Your offers are appreciated.

When we arrived home in Iron River, a phone message told us that someone wanted to bring us a complete turkey dinner on thanksgiving. We are not sure whom, the woman who called said that someone had a surplus from their garden and wanted to share. People are wonderful. Cory Holsclaw had us plowed out and I had to shovel about 3-5 inches from our sidewalk to get into the house, but I also need the exercise so that was good for me.

We both are humbled by 398 visits to this site. Words cannot express how grateful we are for the support we are receiving on this journey.

Thank you. Karen

Saturday, November 27, 2010 7:19 AM, CST

Good news this morning. First day after his 1st chemo treatment. Dan woke up without gasping for breath - he went upstairs, did a few things before using his nebulizer—this is first time since October 22nd he could breath easy upon arising from bed. His cough is better, and the back rib pain from deep coughing is gone. No change in voice yet but we are very hopeful. All the prayers and chemo are working to make his life easier. Praise the Lord! The photo I am using is of Dan in 1960 water-skiing with our friends on White Bear Lake where he and his family lived for many years.

Saturday, November 27, 2010 8:07 PM, CST

Our family would like to say thanks to all with their comments and prayers since dad's diagnosis and the beginning of his Chemo treatments this past week. This next week mom and dad will be moving to Duluth in an effort to reduce their driving through the snow this winter. Mom and dad welcome visitors to their condo but all visitors must be healthy. The weekly Chemo treatments affect dad's immune system making him unable to fight off even the common cold. Anyone that has a fever, cough, cold, flu or any other illness please send an email and stop by when you are feeling better. Thank you again and keep the prayers coming!

Dan Collins (Son)

Sunday, November 28, 2010 3:25 PM, CST

A special Thank You to Kitty and Lee Ruska for taking over our Homebound Communion program. We have one lovely lady that we have been bringing Communion to for almost three years and she is unable to get out of her home except for doctor appointments and that is painful for her. She has a friendly, positive attitude and we have grown to love her. We brought communion to her every week unless we were out of town and she always was very appreciative of our visits. We received a letter from her when we came home from Duluth telling us that Kitty and Lee are now bringing her communion. I called Kitty and asked her if she would notify the church office for us to let them know they had to find someone to take over for us. We are so happy to learn that they volunteered to do this. We are blessed to have your friendship and you will also be a blessing to her.

Thanks so much Kitty & Lee.

Wednesday, December 1, 2010 12:37 PM, CST

HOME SWEET HOME. We are now settled in to our new home in Duluth. Dan and Ann Collins have been with us since Saturday and we moved in yesterday, one day earlier than we originally planned. The move went very well. They did all the work – since Dan is not very strong, there was no way I could have moved us in here without them! Not only moving, they cooked and cleaned every day in Iron River to help us close the house. Our first night here, they cooked us a delicious shrimp scampi dinner. We thank God every day for blessing us with wonderful caring children. Dan and Ann left to go home to Appleton, WI this morning.

The condo is beautiful, we are thoroughly enjoying the views of Lake Superior and watching the large ore boats sailing in front of our windows day and night. It is quiet here day and night – that was one of our concerns as we are use to quiet days and nights at the lake. We were concerned it would be too noisy for us in the city. This place is every bit as quiet as it is on Buskey Bay in Iron River. We also sure enjoy the underground heated parking. Haven't tried the pool yet but will soon. Dan has been advised to exercise as much as possible so we will also make use of the Fitness Center.

The staff here at Beacon Pointe Resort is very good to us. Stephanie Olsen, the Manager, has been outstanding and ready to help us with everything. Did you know they rent out rooms here if you are visiting the area? We highly recommend it—you cannot believe the views of Lake Superior, and how nice it is, until you see it. We were surprised to hear you can rent a room for overnight or a weekend.

This week our schedule is as follows:

Dec. 2 – Surgery at Miller-Dwan to put in a port.

Dec. 3 – 2nd Chemotherapy.

Dec. 4 – Son Joe arrives from Two Rivers to spend a week
with us.

Sunday, December 5, 2010 7:00 PM, CST

Sorry I did not update this journal earlier this week. My only excuse is that the week went by like a flash. Dan and Ann left on Wednesday morning. They had us all settled in nicely before leaving and we are so thankful they could be here. Dan had his port put in at Miller-Dwan Outpatient Surgery on Thursday and that went well. The port will save his veins since they can take all his blood draws through the port and the chemo can be done through the port also. On Friday, he had his second chemotherapy. We spent 5 hours at the clinic as he also had a visit with a Nurse Practitioner who was very informative and prescribed some new meds for him. Mary Lou was also with us and we sure appreciate that she is doing this. She remembers things to ask that we don't and is always a calming influence on both of us during this time.

Dan has a very deep cough and it gives him a great deal of pain in the chest, ribs and back so the NP prescribed new meds for it. So far, they help a little but they have not taken the pain away when he coughs, so he still has a sore chest, ribs and back even though he is on morphine. On Friday night, our son, Pat and Tambrey, came over and Pat cooked a delicious dinner for us. On Saturday, the day after chemo, Dan felt pretty good. We attended 4:30 pm Mass at the Cathedral as we figured that it would be less crowded than Sunday. The first day after both chemo treatments are the best days for him, then day two and three are not so good. Our son, Joe, arrived last night, Mary Lou picked him up at the airport and he stayed in Superior with them since it was late. Today we all enjoyed a delicious turkey dinner at their home in Superior. Dan did pretty well today but the cough started up again tonight, and the pain came back. Joe will be staying here with us all this week to help us out. We are so thankful for his help. We may go to Iron River tomorrow if Dan is feeling better to pick up more things we need and to finish closing down the house for the winter. It is good for us to do things when Dan is feeling up to it and he wants to go to Iron River. Joe will do all the shoveling that is needed. The driveway is being plowed for us and our neighbor, Barb Gillis, tells us they had a fluffy snow today but that we should have no problems getting in. Our next chemo is Friday and we see Dr. Lalich at that appointment which is good because we have many questions for him. We are still very comfortable in our condo at Beacon Pointe. The staff here is very good to us. We made the right decision in coming here and it is such a relief to be close to the clinic and to our children up here. No worries about snow or driving, as we are ten minutes from the clinic. The photo I am using tonight is one that Dan and Ann took in our living room. You can see Lake Superior right behind us. We enjoy our view better than TV.

Friday, December 10, 2010 4:32 PM, CST

Today Dan finished his first cycle (3 treatments-once a week) of chemotherapy. Next week he has a week off and his second cycle was changed to Wednesday instead of Friday so he has more than a week off. He is looking forward to that very much. His days are up and down, however, the last three days were good. We are giving him his medications on a proactive basis instead of reactive and thus we are staying ahead of the pain, and other side effects as much as possible. His weight stayed level this past week, the week before he had lost about 5 lbs and cannot afford to continue doing that so we were happy with his weigh in today. Next week, he is scheduled for a swallowing test at the hospital as an outpatient, and an ENT specialist appointment to examine the paralyzed vocal cord. They may do a short operational procedure to move the cord to the position it should be which should stop the aspirating episodes he is having every so often. It may also help bring his voice back, we hope, but no promises on that. Today we had an appointment with his oncologist, Dr. Lalich and he was pleased with the progress so far. Dan asked him how long he has had the tumor. He told us probably a year, but since there were no symptoms, a chest CT scan was not done. If it had been, it would have been seen and he told us that is why most lung cancer is advanced by the time it is found. For those of you who do not know, Dan smoked in his late high school years, through his army years and continued until 1974 when he quit. Even though he has not had a cigarette for 36-years, it did its damage. Dr. Lalich will order a CT scan after the second cycle is completed and that will show us if the chemotherapy is working. He feels optimistic that it is working.

Our son, Joe from Two Rivers, has been here helping us all week and he has been very busy helping us make our new place a home with many trips to the store and working around the condo. He remodeled an empty closet by installing an expandable rod and shoe stand so we have another closet. All done without any nails on the walls. He made arrangements to pick up Dan's sister, Peg Likar, who lives in Duluth so she could visit us here. He also drove us back to Iron River to close down the house and pick up some things we forgot and went to the doctor's appointment today with us. We are so thankful he was able to be here. Mary Lou was also at the chemo appointment after Joe left to go home. Dan and I want to thank everyone for the caring thoughts, words and prayers you sent us in the mail and on the guest book. It is a joy for Dan and I to read them and we appreciate your love and concern. It is a difficult time, and especially during this holiday season, however, we both know the true meaning of Christmas and that is what we focus on every day. Our family celebrates this holy season every year together and this year we will do it on the weekend of January 8 and 9th. We (all 18 of us) are going to Wisconsin Dells to the Kalahara Resort. Today we were able to adjust Dan's chemo the week before the trip on Tuesday so we hope that he will be strong enough to make the trip. The first two days after chemo are the most difficult for him. The picture I am using today is of Joe and his Dad on our deck. They had a great time watching the boats this week also.

Saturday, December 11, 2010 5:49 AM, CST

And she still is watching over her Dad every day through his battle with lung cancer with the same love in her eyes.

Saturday, December 11, 2010 5:34 PM, CST

In November of 1984, Dan was diagnosed with rectal cancer. At that time, his doctor told me that he had a 50% chance of living for more than 5 years. During recuperation after his surgery, he did this cross-stitching of Footprints in the Sand. That is why I chose this background for the Caring Bridge website. I am posting a photo of this cross-stitch that he did back then. That was the only picture he wanted to take to our new condo. It is hanging over our dining room table now. I think everyone will see the depth of his faith and his love in the Lord when looking at the beautiful job he did and knowing how he wanted it brought to Duluth for his new battle with cancer.

I was asked to post our address and zip code as I missed the zip code when done earlier so here is where we are living:

Dan & Karen Collins
Beacon Pointe Resort
2100 Water StreetUnit #202
Duluth MN 55812

Tuesday, December 14, 2010 7:06 AM, CST

Some of you do not know that I have been cutting Dan's hair for almost 50 years (our anniversary 9-9-61). He tells me he has only had 2 professional cuts in all those years. I also cut all the kids hair until they wouldn't let me do it any more but Dan always liked my haircuts. This morning I had to do one that no one really wants to do but he has been shedding hair every day and it was beginning to bother him so we had a hair cutting session. I gave him a buzz. I was concerned about cutting it bald in fear of cutting him. His first words were - "This reminds me of my first cut in the Army". I used my smallest attachment and if falling hair continues to bother him, I will use his electric razor. He was told not to use a blade on his face or head during this time. I think he is as handsome as ever! Yes, we have some winter caps with us! We were prepared for this but it is still not easy.

Tuesday, December 14, 2010 9:30 PM, CST

Since Dan's last chemo on Friday, he has been doing pretty well. Meds are helping with side effects. The swallowing test at the hospital on Monday went well and he has an ENT appointment tomorrow to check out the paralyzed vocal cord. After that test, our grandson, Nate, drove me out to Iron River for some banking, to check in at the house and helped to bring more things up here. He shoveled our path and there was about 4 inches of snow. Dan decided to stay in Duluth since we had several stops to make. This morning Dan was well enough to go out to the mall to make two quick stops. Tonight Nate brought dinner over and spent the evening with us and he will be back to cook for us tomorrow night. We are being spoiled. Nate is a fine cook and a very caring grandson. For those who do not know, he is Dan and Ann's son from Appleton and is attending nursing college up here this year. He is living with Mary Lou and Don in Superior. The photo I am using of Nate and Dan is the first photo since the new hair cut early this morning. It is nice for both of us to have a whole week without a chemo treatment. Hopefully, he will feel stronger every day this week.

Sunday, December 19, 2010 8:25 AM, CST

Dan and I want to wish all of you a Merry Christmas and a Happy New Year. He's had a very good week since his last chemo treatment on December 10th. He begins his second cycle of treatment on December 22nd. We've had many wonderful visits with our family this week and look forward to more family holiday gatherings this coming week. Our photo is our only holiday decoration this year. Thank you to everyone for your prayers and your wonderful words of encouragement and support. We have decided not to send individual Christmas cards this year-we hope everyone understands.

Love to all, Dan and Karen

Monday, December 20, 2010 5:55 AM, CST

We had a wonderful day yesterday. In the morning, Pat & Tambrey came to visit us. Pat has been suffering with a cold for a week so he stayed away from his Dad, but is now over it. They brought over a tripod and a hunter's spotting scope so we can use it over the lake. We will be enjoying a crossword puzzle they also gave us of Lake Superior, which fits perfectly on our coffee table. After attending a beautiful 1:00 PM Mass at St. Mary's Hospital, we were invited for dinner at Don and Mary Lou's in Superior and enjoyed time with them and Logan, Kalen and Nate. Dan had three helpings of Mary Lou's delicious Beef Stroganoff! It was our first "night" trip and coming back home the lights of Duluth and Bentleyville were awesome.

Thursday, December 23, 2010 8:42 PM, CST

Cycle-2 began on Wednesday and several changes were made to the Chemo plans. Dad now has thrombocytopenia, which is a drop in his platelets; platelets are needed for the blood to clot. Due to this drop they have changed the frequency of the Carboplatin. The Carboplatin is the cause of the drop and he was getting it in a large dose on the first chemo treatment of the cycle, now he will be getting it each week in smaller doses with the weekly paclitaxel which the Oncologist's state will have a lesser effect on Dads platelets. This change also now has dad getting Chemo every week rather than having the fourth week off. On Wednesday the Oncologist also adjusted his anti-nausea medications and from what we saw already this week has had a positive impact. I was glad to see how good dad was feeling this week and his continued positive attitude! His sister Peg and two of her kids, Mary Starkman and Mike Likar and his wife, Midori, also visited him this week.

I enjoyed the visit also as it had been years since I have seen Mike.

Thanks to all of you that continue to send comments and well wishes via this site, it really means a lot to all of us and all the prayers have already been showing results.

Merry Christmas and Happy New Year, Dan (son)

Tuesday, December 28, 2010 7:43 AM, CST

Dan's had a very good week after his Chemo treatment last Wednesday. The new formula as outlined in our last journal entry done by our son, Dan, helped the side effects. We had many wonderful visits with family through Christmas and this week we are expecting: John and Sue McLennan and Gale and Julie Mellum, who

are long time lake friends from Karen's high school days on the lake. We are happy that they all still have homes on the Pike Lake Chain in Iron River, and that we all continue to treasure our friendships, including how happy we are that our spouses all enjoy being together as well. My sister, Mary Peterson, will also be arriving for New Year's Eve, weather permitting. We are looking forward to all the visits this week. On Wednesday, Dan will have chemotherapy again - this week we do not see Dr. Lalich, however, he was there if we needed him.

We thank everyone for all their prayers; as Danny said in the last journal entry, they are working. Dan feels so much better than he did two months ago when all this started. His breathing is so much better and he does not use the albuterol by nebulizer any more, only a maintenance drug for breathing is required. No more pain in his ribs, chest or back! He is sleeping well. His taste buds are still pretty well gone, however, sometimes they recover for a tasty meal. He still does not have his voice back. He whispers as loud as he can. All and all, life is less painful for him right now than it was in October and November. Things started to improve right after the first chemo treatment and from all the prayers across this country, and even from Mexico and Montenegro where friends are praying. Words cannot express our appreciation for your caring thoughts, words, and prayers. Please continue to pray for him. Thank you.

The photo used today is of Dan wearing the new treasured Viking cap that the Griffith family had in his stocking Christmas morning, along with other treats. He also received a handmade bookmark from his granddaughter, Kalen Griffith, that reads, Vikings are strong just like you Grandpa! You are right Kalen—he is strong and the bookmark is used every day as he continues to enjoy reading daily.

Tuesday, January 4, 2011 5:31 AM, CST

Today begins Dan's first chemo treatment in the New Year. Hopefully, it will not be as long as last Wednesday as there was a lab error with his blood and we were there from 12:15 PM to 5:45. They assure us that will not happen again. Dan has not been feeling well since Saturday. The anti nausea medication did not prevent it and he was unable to keep down his food. Yesterday he started a new prescription that is the same drug they give him along with the chemo and it lasts for 48 hours. After the 48 hours, he starts the nausea, so the Dr. wants to continue it by mouth to see if it helps Dan avoid all that he experienced this past week. This morning he is feeling better. The past three days he has not been able to eat much except ensure, crackers and soup. That worries me, as he cannot afford to lose more weight. Last night, after the new med, he was able to eat a normal meal and did not lose it. We move forward now with hope in our hearts that the New Year will improve for him. The treatment is one day earlier this week because our family holiday gathering is this weekend in the Dells. We plan to drive there on Friday morning and return on Sunday. All 18 of our family plan to be there and Dan and I are looking forward to it very much. Thank you for your prayers - please keep them coming! May you all have a Happy, Blessed and Healthy New Year. God Bless you all.

Monday, January 10, 2011 4:03 PM, CST

We had a very busy week. It started with Dan having chemo treatment on Tuesday, January 4 and that went very well. No more problems with the blood. His platelets are up and the treatment lasted only 3 1/2 hours. He did not have the nausea problems that he had last week-this week has been much better. The new meds and prayers helped him very much and we thank you all for your continued prayers. On Thursday, we had a great visit with Karen's cousin and his wife, Tom and Marsha Bouchard from Ashland.

On Friday morning, our grandson, Nate, drove us to Wisconsin Dells to Kalahari Resort for our holiday celebration with the family. We all had a wonderful time, the resort was absolutely beautiful and you will see some pictures soon of the large slide that Dan climbed WAY up and rode down with Mary Lou while the other family watched them land at the end! He is amazing. We also used a tube along the lazy river and our children and grandchildren did everything from rock climbing, golfing in Wisconsin in the winter, surf boarding and rides on an indoor Ferris Wheel. Dan handled the whole trip great and we enjoyed spending this time with all our family as that does not happen too often with 18 of us, five grand-kids in college with jobs, and the other three in sport events this time of the year. We are so happy that our children make this happen every year when they are all so busy with their work and family life. We highly recommend the resort to everyone. The place is marvelous and we were very comfortable in the condo. A shuttle carried us back and forth to the water and theme parks as often as we wanted-it even drove some of us to the Tangier Mall right next door. We never moved our car while there. We also had a wonderful visit with Karen's cousin, Mary Lou (Bouchard) Hudack and her husband, Larry, who live in the Dells. We returned home on Sunday. Nate drove very well, there were two flipped cars on our way down Friday, and it did not faze him a bit. He said it was inattentive driving!

Wednesday, January 19, 2011 5:00 PM, CST

From Footprints in the Sand: During your time of trials & suffering, when you see only one set of footprints on the sand, it was then that "I" carried you. The Lord carried Dan the past two months and "He" heard all the prayers from friends and family.

Fourth Stage Lung Cancer diagnosed on 11/19 and we were told a life expectancy of 4 months without chemo, 8 months with chemo is the average. We told the Doctor at that point that God can change that prognosis and he agreed. On Monday this week, Dan had the first CT Scan after 7 chemo treatments. Today, Joe, Mary Lou, Dan and I met with Dr. Lalich and he told us the malignant tumor is gone - the nodes are gone from both lungs. He said that if the Radiologist did not have the Nov. 19th scan, his report would state that these lungs are free of cancer. Dr. Lalich said this is amazing and not the normal outcome. We said it was a miracle and also because of a great doctor and all the prayers across the world.

The doctor said it is not a cure. Lung Cancer, like breast cancer cells is not cured by chemo but they do go into remission and that is what has happened. The plan is to give Dan two more treatments this month, then a week off, and then three more weeks and another CT will be done. If it is the same as the current scan, he will stop the chemo for two months and let Dan recuperate from the treatments and take another scan at the end of those two months. Please continue to keep Dan in your prayers. You are all responsible for this wonderful news.

God bless you all and thank you again from all our family.

Tuesday, January 25, 2011 10:00 AM, CST

Dan's had a busy week since our last Chemo treatment and great news on Wednesday, January 19th. On Thursday, our son, Joe drove us to Iron River to look over our home and we visited with our neighbors and friends, Howard Furhmann and Barb Gillis. We also stopped in to see our friends at Security State Bank. On Friday, we went to North Country Independent Living at UWS where they helped Dan select a voice amplifier, which will assist with the telephone as well as being portable so he can wear it. We continue to pray and wait for the paralyzed vocal cord to heal now that the tumor is gone and that the thickening around that area is reduced. We were told he would know in three months if it works or not. If not, surgery and/or injections will be needed.

Starting Friday afternoon, Dan has suffered with nausea, which did not end until Monday evening. Dr. Lalich has changed course again with it, using new meds by mouth, and stopping the meds he gave him with chemo last week to prevent it since it actually lasted longer than usual this time. Dan could not eat much since Friday so I am concerned about his weight again, however, he has a 13-day break after chemo tomorrow so he can work at eating more during that time. Hopefully, the nausea will not be as bad this time. Thank you for your continual prayers—we appreciate them so much.

Sunday, January 30, 2011 6:16 PM, CST

Dan is suffering again after the chemotherapy on Wednesday. New meds are still not working. Started getting sick on Friday afternoon and still going on. We will be calling the doctor again tomorrow. He is hoping the doctor will think it best to stop the treatments and do the scan this week. Will keep the site updated with his decision.

Monday, January 31, 2011 7:00 PM, CST

Dan received IV Fluids and anti-nausea medication by IV this afternoon after a good visit with a Nurse Practitioner. Our doctor was in the Ashland office but she was in contact with him about Dan's nausea. He is feeling better tonight and had some dinner. She thought he was dehydrated even though his blood numbers were in the low normal. Other symptoms he had showed he needed to have IV fluids. She also prescribed a different prescription to take at home.

As we turn our new family calendar to February tonight, we are thankful for all the blessings received this past month and for the prayers Dan received from all of you. Our granddaughter, Paige, made this calendar for us and every month has different photos of the family. We love it. Thanks again, Paige.

Tuesday, February 1, 2011 8:58 AM, CST

A quick update—the procedure yesterday worked, as Dan is feeling much better this morning. He not only ate breakfast but also cooked it for both of us! We now will work on gaining some weight, him not me! Dan has lost 13.1 pounds since he started his treatment - that is not good news. Good news is that I have lost 10 lbs.

Sunday, February 6, 2011 3:08 PM, CST

Dan's had a pretty good week since he had the IV's on Monday and a new prescription added to his meds. He had a couple bouts of nausea but not severe and the pill helped. A side effect of the new med, however, is tiredness and he is very tired most of the day, and when I ask him how he is feeling, he says, just blah! He is sleeping every afternoon and goes to bed early. I guess if we have to choose between nausea and being unable to keep his food down to being sleepy and blah, we will take the latter.

We did get out to Mass today - we are going to St. Mary's Chapel in the hospital at 1 PM on Sundays. We enjoy it very much, park in the ramp, all the walking is indoors, and Dan is not exposed to crowds.

Dan and I had several very nice visits this week. His sister, Peg Likar, came over with her son Andy and daughter Carly. Andy is the new Chef at Sir Benedict's in Duluth. Peg moved to Duluth from Ely and lives in the Westwood Senior Apartments on the St. Scholastica campus. Then we had another nice visit with Peg and her daughter, Mary Starkman who is an RN at St. Mary's. Our grandson, Nate Collins, also came and stayed with us one night. We enjoyed his visit and I enjoyed a swim in the pool and hot tub with him also. We also had nice visits with our daughter, Mary Lou, and son, Pat, this week so the week went by quickly for us.

On Wednesday this coming week, Dan has an appointment with

Dr. Lalich to go over the upcoming treatments. He is scheduled for three more chemo treatments. The doctor sent us a message through his nurse last week that he will reduce one of the chemo's (the one causing the nausea) 25%, and schedule him for IV fluids and intravenous anti-nausea meds on Friday following his treatment for the final three treatments. A CT scan will be done in the next few weeks to be sure the results continue to show that the cancer is in remission. After three treatments, we should have a break of two months before another scan will be done. The chemo has been very difficult for Dan the past three weeks so we will be talking to the Doctor about the pros and cons of stopping the chemo sooner. We are hoping he will order the scan this week or early next week and that it continues to show good news. Thank you for your continued prayers. We appreciate them very much.

Wednesday, February 9, 2011 6:16 PM, CST

Today Dan had an appointment with Dr. Lalich before the chemo treatment was scheduled. As of Sunday evening, Dan's nausea increased and we had to increase his medication to two pills. After increasing the pills, the nausea was somewhat better, but not gone, and Dan starting sleeping all the time. By Monday, his sense of balance became affected, and he almost fell twice this week. He stopped one fall in time by grabbing the counter, and I got to him the other time before he went down. He couldn't eat much and has become very weak since Sunday. After explaining all that to the Doctor, Dan asked him why he needed the last three treatments when the tumor is gone and the cancerous nodes were also gone. The Doctor's answer was that he was doing them to prolong the remission of the cancer but that he thinks the chemo should stop now due to Dan's weak condition. In that they have tried all kinds of meds and he continues to be nauseated, he feels Dan needs time to recover. He has scheduled another Chest CT Scan for Dan on March 25th and we will see him the same day for the results. If all is fine, Dan will be off chemo until further scans show cancer - and that is not going to happen, God willing! Dr. Lalich thinks that Dan should start feeling better within two weeks. He gave him IV fluids for dehydration and nausea instead of chemo today and Dan can return for these fluids again Friday or any time next week if the nausea does not improve. He also gave him another new medicine for the nausea. Mary Lou and Pat were with us for this appointment and we all agreed that this was the best thing to do now.

We thank you for all your support and continued prayers for Dan during this time—words cannot express our appreciation.

Friday, February 18, 2011 3:32 PM, CST

Dan is feeling a little better every day now - the nausea is not completely gone but it really does not begin until later in the day and he thinks part of it is because of his taste buds. He cannot taste most foods, but those foods he does taste and likes, sometimes taste bad, so that causes a feeling of nausea. His last chemo was January 26 so that will be a month next week. Dr. Lalich told Dan he should be feeling better within two months and he should be able to taste his food, and we pray the vocal cord will also work.

We have been out to Iron River twice this week, the first time; we found our furnace off due to the batteries going out on our new thermostat. We forgot about the necessity of changing those. As soon as we fixed them, all was fine. We went back today to be sure the furnace was working and everything was fine and we could not believe how much snow had melted in three days since we had been there. No problems on freeze up as we drained all the lines and put in antifreeze before we left in November. It was great to take two trips on two beautiful days this week.

I went to St. Luke's Hospital this afternoon and had a nice visit with Karen Wicklund, a long time high school friend and co-worker at the bank. She is recovering from colon surgery and she looked very good and hopes to go home to Iron River tomorrow.

I will update this site only once a week now that treatments are over unless there is something that I think you would all like to know. Our next doctor visit is on March 25.

Monday, February 28, 2011 7:33 PM, CST

We are happy to begin the month of March with good news about Dan. His nausea is gone; he is eating better and getting stronger every day. He is using the treadmill and the hand weights to help build up his strength and we are going out to walk several times a week. In the cold weather, we are walking through the downtown skywalk system and through the stores. His paralyzed vocal cord is giving some signs of movement - most mornings now he can say a few words without whispering. It does not last too long but it is a good sign. His taste buds are still not back to normal, however, some foods are starting to taste good to him but not too many yet. The doctor told him the taste buds should return in about two months from the end of chemo and he has one month to go.

On March 25th, Dan will have a chest CT Scan to find out if his lungs are still clear of cancer. We are thinking positive thoughts about this test.

On the weekend of April 9th, we plan to move back to Iron River with the help of all our children. We are both looking forward to going home even though we are happy with our Duluth home.

Beacon Pointe has been great for us this winter—the staff here is wonderful, and all the amenities have been very nice. We have enjoyed the heated, underground parking, the pool, hot tub, and fitness center, and the awesome views of Lake Superior. We would not hesitate to stay here again-the condo is very comfortable and well furnished and equipped.

I will not update this website until March 26, after the chest CT Scan so you will all know those results. Thank you for your continued prayers for Dan's recovery-we appreciate it very much.

Monday, March 14, 2011 3:01 PM, CDT

This is a quick update to let you all know that Dan is doing much better. He is eating well and his taste buds are starting to return. We look forward to receiving good news on March 25th when he has his Chest CT Scan. He will also see his ENT Specialist to look at his vocal cord and the Cancer Specialist on the 25th. We will not update the site again until right after those appointments. Thank you for your continued prayers - we appreciate them very much. They are helping. We are also looking forward to moving back home again the weekend of April 9th.

Friday, March 25, 2011 8:18 AM, CDT

PLEASE remember Dan in your prayers today. Chest CT Scan at 2:30 PM today. Will update all of you tonight.

Thank you

Friday, March 25, 2011 4:15 PM, CDT

We have so much to be thankful for again today. The Chest CT Scan shows the cancer is gone. Mary Lou was with us today when we met with Dr. Lalich and he said Dan's lungs look even better than in January. That is the first time he told us the cancer was in remission and how unusual it was for a stage 4 (advanced) lung cancer to go in remission that quickly. Dan's next CT scan will be the end of June (3 months). Words cannot express how thankful we are to God and to all of you for being there with us, for prayers, and for all the support shown to Dan and I, and to all our family. We are heading out to Iron River this weekend and plan to stay until Monday morning.

Friday, April 1, 2011 9:31 AM, CDT

Happy April 1st. This morning when I got up, Dan told me we got six inches of snow and I was pretty disappointed and then he said "April Fools" so you know he still has his sense of humor. We were going to head to Iron River to get mail and move more things in until we called our neighbor Barb Gillis. She told me it was snowing hard and we should wait until tomorrow so we will follow her advice.

It was pointed out to me that I did not mention Dan's paralyzed vocal cord in last journal entry. We did see the ENT specialist, Kim Lakhan, and she said it might take up to six months to repair the nerve. Good signs are that the swelling is all gone and that one lower portion of the vocal cords is moving slightly and it was not moving previously. Dan still cannot talk without a whisper but his amplifier is helping and we tell him he looks pretty cool with the speaker on his ear and mouth. Told him it looks like he is pretty important with an immediate phone connection - I think he is pretty important without it too. Dan wants to give the nerve a chance to heal naturally so he will not undergo any surgery until he is assured that it will not come back without surgery. When you see him, you can expect the speaker and be prepared as sometimes it squeals and he cannot help that! Thank you again for all your comforting words on our guest book and for your many prayers. We will keep you updated with any further news.

Saturday, April 9, 2011 6:27 AM, CDT

We are home in Iron River. Arrived yesterday morning, one day earlier than originally planned. Weather was gorgeous between 65-70 degrees. Our sons, Joe and Dan, and daughter, Mary Lou, moved us back. Son, Pat, was ready to help on our original move date (Saturday), but since he had meetings yesterday, his wife Tambrey was standing by ready to help us. Since we had moved many things during the last month, the move went quickly and we were on our way home by 10:30 AM. When we arrived, we were happy to see Dan and Joe had set up our deck with all the furniture and we were able to enjoy that wonderful sun. Dan Sr. was very busy inside and outside.

He is feeling very good and will become stronger every day now that he is home again and will be outside getting exercise.

This will be our last post. Thank you to everyone for following our journey and for all the prayers and support for Dan and our family. We will never forget it. We are also thankful to the Lord for His many blessings. He will watch over us in the future as He has in the past. May God bless all of you!

Monday, May 23, 2011 12:51 PM, CDT

On May 11, Dan visited with Dr. Lalich due to health concerns. He was having more difficulty breathing, chest discomfort, sleeplessness, and continued weight loss and back pain. The doctor ordered a chest x-ray in advance of the appointment and then after the examination, he sent him over to the hospital for a CT Scan of the lungs. He was concerned about blood clots and/or a change in the remission of cancer.

The CT Scan showed an increased size of a pulmonary nodule in the left lung base from a size of 2mm to a 7mm and development of a new nodule (size 7mm) in the right lower lobe. There is an unchanged 1.4 cm right node. Given the history of lung cancer, the radiologist and Dr. Lalich treat these nodes as being metastatic (cancerous). There were no blood clots.

Dan had stopped taking the morphine when the prescription ran out as we both thought it was mainly for his back and it was doing better. The Doctor said he should not have stopped taking it, as it was also to help with breathing, chest discomfort, and sleeping as well as back pain. After beginning the morphine again, all of his symptoms disappeared, he started sleeping well, breathing better and the pain is gone in his chest and even his back pain is much better. Thank God!

Dr. Lalich has started Dan on an oral chemo drug called Tarceva. He takes one tablet a day. Normal side effects are rash and possible loose bowels. This drug is known to inhibit and stabilize the cancerous nodes. The doctor was optimistic that it will help Dan without starting chemotherapy at this time.

He started the pill on Tuesday, May 17th and so far no side effects. The medicine will lower his resistance to infection. He needs to prevent infection by avoiding contact with people with colds and other infections so we have to ask our family and friends not to visit us if they are suffering from colds and infections. He will be careful in crowds by carrying and using a hand sanitizer.

Dan is scheduled to return to see the doctor on June 8 and another CT scan in July. One other problem he still endures is loss of taste buds. He can taste foods, however, most foods do not taste very good to him. It seems that spicy foods taste better and he needs more salt than normal. This problem seems to have increased after starting the Tarceva but it did not start the problem, as it never really went away after his chemotherapy this winter. He continues to have a problem with his paralyzed vocal cord, however, his voice is no longer a whisper, and he has not used his amplifier for some time. His voice is very hoarse and at sometimes very weak.

We appreciate your continued prayers for Dan as he courageously fights this disease. Thank you.

Wednesday, July 13, 2011 9:15 PM, CDT

Dan had several appointments today at SMDC Cancer Center, Lab, Fluid and Med Infusion, CAT Scan and an appointment with Dr. Lalich.

The CAT Scan showed no improvement since Dan started the oral chemo drug (Tarceva) on May 17th. He used this drug for thirty days and had to stop as he became very sick. The CAT Scan also showed additional pulmonary nodules in the lungs since the May scan, and a new cyst growth probably associated with the emphysema. The nodules found on the last scan were larger this time but the Doctor said none of them are too bad yet. He suggested giving Dan more time to get his strength back and then begin regular chemo treatments again. Dan told the Doctor that chemo treatments are no longer an option. He does not want any more treatments, as he cannot have any quality in his life on chemo. Dr. Lalich understood his feelings and respects his decision.

In that Dan is also experiencing more breathing difficulties, he gave him another medication for that and an anti-depressant medication to help him with every day stress situations that occur for all patients enduring this disease.

Dr. Lalich also ordered Hospice in our home for Dan. He told us that this cancer is terminal and the prognosis is that he may live a few months or several months. He cannot give us any positive time and we realized that. The Hospice nurse will probably see Dan only once a week while he is feeling well, more often as he needs it. The CAT Scans will not continue as these are done to help the doctor decide on the type of Chemotherapy needed for treatment. Dr. Lalich will continue overseeing his care and will see Dan every two months. He will also continue his weekly infusion of liquids and anti nausea meds as long as they are helping Dan to feel better.

That pretty well sums up our long day - from 8:30 to 5:30 at the clinic today. We ask for your continued prayers for Dan and appreciate them very much. It is all in God's hands—we have known that all along and we are ready to accept His will in this journey. We pray for strength to do this.

Love to all, Karen and Dan

Friday, July 22, 2011 5:26 AM, CDT

We will try to update this site weekly so all of you know how Dan is doing. The number of emails, guest book entries, calls and cards we are receiving humbles us. We also appreciate all the offers to help us. We are so thankful for Al Nicol, our neighbor and friend, who cuts our grass every week. Many "Angels" are touching us in our lives. Al is one of them.

Even though we spent most of the past week in the air conditioning, we had a busy week. On Tuesday, the Hospice Staff from St. Mary's in Duluth came to our home and were here for almost six hours. The social worker and case manager came separately. They have a team approach to their care, everyone from the Doctors, Social Workers, Bereavement counselors, nurses, health aides, therapists and nutritional specialists. Dr. Lalich recommended Dan to Hospice on July 13th. We received a call from the nurse manager Wednesday morning following a team meeting at the hospital regarding Dan's condition. The doctor made some changes to his medication based on the symptoms he is experiencing. The nurse will come once a week until more visits are needed. Dan is not on oxygen but they wanted it on hand so both stationery and portable tanks were delivered on Wednesday and we learned how to operate them. Yesterday we returned to the clinic for his weekly fluid and anti-nausea infusion. Dan is feeling pretty good right now, he is two months off of the Tarceva (oral chemo) and the longer the time off, the better he is feeling. Some days are better for him than other days, so we take one day at a time, thankful for the good days. He may be able to stop these weekly infusions, but he is approved for them as long as they help him feel better. Yesterday, he said, "I think that I may prove the Doctor wrong about this diagnosis!"

Words cannot express how much we appreciate the staff at SMDC's Cancer Center. When we go there, it is like we are family. Dr. Lalich, his nurses and the infusion staff are all very professional and yet make us feel like we are with friends and family. Even though the rooms are filled with patients, they make us feel like we are special to them. They are also Angels on earth.

We both feel this is too early for Hospice, but we learned from their staff that this is the ideal time to get started. It is a relief to have someone in charge of all the medication, as it has been difficult having the prescriptions filled as some days it is too early and we even had both Walgreen and Wal-Mart run out of his breathing meds. One day I had to make calls all morning to find it and then had to worry whether it would arrive in time or should we drive up to get it. Now all meds are ordered by the nurse and delivered the next day.

We enjoy Mass and coffee at St. Michael every Tuesday, Wednesday and Friday morning and have a wonderful group of friends there.

Dan has attended daily Mass ever since his rectal cancer in 1984. Father Mike makes the Mass a very devout, wonderful experience and we are blessed to be able to participate. Dan says "It lifts my spirit" and I agree with this wholeheartedly.

We thank God for all of you and your prayers. The Lord continues to keep us in the palm of His Hand and we are feeling His presence daily.

Thursday, July 28, 2011 5:03 PM, CDT

A quick update: Dan is doing okay, had a busy two weeks with visits from Hospice: Nurse, Bereavement Counselor, call from Spiritual Counselor, and two visits from Midwest Medical Supply. He is sleeping well, very little pain, and is eating, however, appetite not so good. Supplementing meals with Carnation Breakfast Drink, which tastes better to him than Ensure. Hopefully, he will start eating better soon.

Went up to Duluth today and last Thursday for infusion of liquids and nausea medication. His energy level is not great but we are getting out to Mass & coffee several times during the week and enjoyed an outdoor Mass at Moon Lake said by our Bishop. Thank you all for the guest-book comments, and your prayers. Thanks also for the wonderful cards we have received. We appreciate your thoughtfulness very much.

Friday, August 5, 2011 9:52 AM, CDT

A short update: Dan is doing pretty well. We cancelled his fluid infusion for today as he feels it is not needed. Dan has experienced some new pain on his side so pain medicine has been increased and it is helping. Lots of great visits this week, two of his Cretin High School classmates and their wives came for visits. Charles and Marion Eldridge and George and Kay Rossez. George and Kay spent a night with us. We enjoyed both of these visits very much. This weekend expecting to see all our children here and maybe some grandchildren. The Hospice nurse, Gary Peterson, came on Tuesday and we received a nice call from the Hospice Chaplain who is coming out next week. We even picked raspberries this week for about one hour and made his favorite pie and freezer jam. Thank you for your continued prayers cards and visits.

Monday, August 15, 2011 9:02 AM, CDT

Today I realized it has been ten days since I updated this site. From all the wonderful cards and calls we receive, we know there are many of you near and far away that read this and are praying for Dan, so I will try to be more diligent and update weekly. Hopefully, you will know that no news is sometimes Good News!

If you ask Dan how are you feeling, he will say, "I am ok". He continues with his nebulizer four times a day and other meds, is now eating better. His food is starting to taste like food, and he is no longer going up to the clinic for fluid infusions.

We had a wonderful visit with St. Mary's Hospice Chaplain last week and Dan's nurse is coming out every Tuesday afternoon. With their excellent care in our home, we have decided to stay home for the winter months. Since Dan will not be on chemo, there is no reason we have to live in the Twin Ports. I have learned to run the John Deere and like to shovel snow for exercise. One day soon, we will plan to purchase an electric start snow blower that is small enough for me to operate, yet big enough to take care of the sidewalk when I cannot shovel. We will contract for our driveways to be plowed. We also have a wonderful support system in Iron River and people are always asking us "What can we do for you? So we know our winter will be fine. Iron River is a community with very caring and loving people.

All of our children are coming here often and we are so appreciative of their loving care and feel God has truly blessed us with their lives. They are giving us great support and devoted care while they have full busy lives with jobs and children. All four families have been here within the last two weeks to help and spend time with us. Dan's sister Peg Likar, and her daughter, Mary Starkman, also was here Saturday with lunch, which included delicious Alaskan Salmon that she grilled.

Thank you again everyone for your cards, calls and prayers. Dan is reaping the benefits of all your love and concern.

Tuesday, August 23, 2011 3:24 PM, CDT

Dan is doing okay, eating and sleeping well. Everyone that comes to see us tells him that he looks very good.

A counselor that visited us from Hospice told Dan that he finds that people on hospice do better when they set special goals for themselves - times and events they want to attend. Dan picked September 9th as his first goal, which is our 50th Wedding Anniversary. Plans are now in place for that celebration and we will post some photos of that after the event. Today Dan said he should set another goal since that is right around the corner, so he decided my birthday on October 26th would be his next goal.

Thank you for your continued prayers—Dan is doing better because of them. A quote from the footprints in the sand -"the Lord replied, "My gracious precious child, I love you and would never leave you. During your times of trials and suffering, when you see only one set of footprints, it was then that I carried you," Dan is being carried every day!

Since our last update, we have had many visits from family and friends near and far: My sister, Mary Peterson from Inver Grove Heights, MN, Dan's cousins - John and Janet Ahern from Hudson, WI; my cousins Tom and Marsha Bouchard and Pete and Barb (Bouchard) Galligan from Barksdale (right near Ashland). Also visits with the Chesney family, Gale & Julie Mellum, John & Sue McClennan,

Tom Hoeltgen, Jim Nelson, Al Nicol and Barb Gillis, our lake friends and neighbors. We appreciate all the visits very much. Thank you for coming.

Thursday, September 8, 2011 7:45 AM, CDT

A quick update: Will update this journal on Monday after our busy anniversary weekend. Today Dan has an appointment with Dr. Lalich at SMDC Cancer Center in Duluth. He is doing ok but has increasing breathing difficulties. All our children and most of the grandchildren will be arriving soon for the weekend. Thank you for your continued prayers—we appreciate them very much.

Friday, September 9, 2011 6:59 AM, CDT

"A Marriage made in Heaven," Dan told Karen this morning—we met in Ely, MN in November 1959 when Karen's brother, Don Peterson, married Amy Likar. Dan decided to go deer hunting that weekend and drove to Ely with his sister, Peg Likar and her husband,

Frank Likar. Karen was a bridesmaid in that wedding and so was Peg. Don met Amy on the Great Falls Montana Air Force Base where he was stationed. The first thing we did together was to dance the jitterbug! Our marriage was blessed with four wonderful, loving and caring children and eight grandchildren, along with their wonderful spouses. We thank the Lord for 50 great years!

Sunday, September 11, 2011 5:34 PM, CDT

We met with Dan's oncologist on September 8th. Dr. Lalich was very happy with how Dan looked; his lungs were clear, and his heart sounded good. We discussed his breathing difficulties and he suggested another medicine but wanted to hold off on it for now.

Dan's next appointment is November 8th.

We have posted photos of our anniversary weekend. Before Dan was diagnosed with Lung Cancer, we told our children that we were thinking of a trip to Paris for our 50th anniversary. To our surprise, they set up a beautiful Paris themed anniversary party Saturday night for us, with French shirts, black berets to wear on our head, good wine, delicious food, music and a wonderful time for all. Our grandson also made the famous Collins Wedding Punch, which was made and served at all the weddings in Dan's family, by his father.

Today, we had a beautiful Mass and reception right after Mass. Father Mike gave us a special blessing and our son, Joe, sang Danny Boy during the service. Many friends joined our family and everything was absolutely beautiful. We told our children that the whole weekend was much better than going to Paris and we were so happy to be able to share our joy with all of them. We are so thankful for all they did for us. You will see some of our fun by looking at the new photos posted today. Thanks to all of you for your continued prayers, calls, cards.

Thursday, September 22, 2011 3:18 PM, CDT

Dan started using oxygen 24/7 this past week. Portable oxygen tanks were delivered in three sizes so he can carry a smaller one when we go to church for Mass or any short trips. A large refill concentrator was delivered also so we can refill these tanks, which makes it very convenient. He has 25+ ft of tubing to the home oxygen unit so he can stay connected in all our main rooms.

The Hospice Nurse was here on Tuesday and heard the change in his lungs. Up to this week, the lungs were clear when examined, however, now every time he breathes out, the Nurse could hear noises in his lungs. We don't remember what he called the noise, but the good news is that he did not hear any fluid sounds. Sometimes, Dan is also having difficulty swallowing so he has to eat very slowly and be very careful chewing and swallowing pills.

We appreciate all your continued prayers for him. Thank you.

Friday, September 30, 2011 8:12 AM, CDT

Yesterday Dan met with his Otolaryngology Specialist at SMDC in Duluth (Kimberly Lakhan, PA-C) as he continues to have swallowing difficulty. She treated his paralyzed vocal cord and her last exam was in December. The exam showed that his paralyzed cord is moving slightly allowing the other cord to reach over and allows him to have a voice. The swelling is all gone and it looked much better than it did in December. She said that everything he told her about the swallowing indicates that he has Esophageal Dysphagia or Zenker's Diverticulum. In layman's language, he has a pocket that his food will sometime go into preventing him from swallowing it. When Dan massages his throat, he eventually moves it out of the pocket and the food goes down. This is painful for him whenever it happens. She was unable to see the pocket with the scope used and she said a barium swallow with x-rays is necessary to determine the severity of the pocket. She explained the treatments for a severe condition and it included surgery and in the worse case scenario is insertion of a feeding tube. The least invasive treatment is to work harder lubricating his food as it goes down, drinking lots of fluids, before, during and after eating. One of his problems is that sometimes fluid also becomes stuck in the pocket. Dan decided he wanted to try increasing the fluids before doing the barium swallow. He does not want surgery and feeding tubes. I already started to serve softer foods more often in our diet once his swallowing difficulty started which was a few weeks ago. The swallowing and breathing difficulties are his daily struggles. Thank you for your continued emails, calls and prayers. The Lord God is truly by our side and carrying both of us through it all.

Thursday, October 6, 2011 7:03 PM, CDT

Dan had his swallowing test on Tuesday and there were no pockets in his esophagus, however, there was a definite narrowing so Dan's ENT specialist got together with his oncologist and they scheduled a CT Scan as they were concerned that something might be pressing on the esophagus to cause this narrowing (suspected tumor). Today he had the CT Scan and thank the Lord, there was no tumor pressing on it, he has a narrowing and that is why he is having trouble getting food to go down. The oncologist called a gastrology doc while we were in his office and they scheduled a scope test on Monday where he will widen the esophagus where it is narrowed, possibly inserting a stent to keep it open. This should help his food go down and may help with the pain he has on his neck, as it may be referred pain.

The CT scan also showed some new nodes and some increase in size of the nodes in his lungs but the Doctor said it is really a very minimal increase at this time. All of this does, however, cause his increased breathing difficulties and the need for continual oxygen.

We are feeling very blessed tonight and Dan said he has been given some more time now. Next appointment with the oncologist is November 8th. Will not update this site until after that appointment. Thanks again for all your prayers, emails and calls. We sure appreciate them very much.

Thursday, October 6, 2011 10:01 PM, CDT

Thanks to Mary Lou, our daughter, for being with us again today for the CT Scan and then for the appointment with the oncologist. You give us great comfort during these appointments.

Wednesday, October 12, 2011 6:07 PM, CDT

Dan has been in the hospital since Monday after he had an esophagus widening procedure with a stent placement. The opening of his esophagus was less that 1/4 inch, it is being widen from approximately 2 mm to 17 mm's. The stent is a smart metal, according to the Doc and will continue working until it has gone to 17mm. Each time it expands, Dan has intense pain in the chest, and the Doc explained that the stent is crushing everything away, to open the pathway, and that includes any nerves in the way. It is amazing he has been able to eat anything with this opening and it sure explains his choking episodes. He is on intravenous morphine with a pump to give him the meds whenever the pain comes, and will be in the hospital until the expansion is completed and pills or liquid morphine can handle the pain. The Doc said he has never seen an opening so small and was hardly able to insert a wire into it - he told us that he thinks there is a mass pressing on the esophagus that caused this, even though the chest CT Scan did not show one. We plan to talk to the Oncologist again to get this info clarified. Today Dan started pureed foods and tolerated them well. We are hoping the switch to pills tonight will work so he can come home tomorrow. The Doc thinks the expansion is almost complete as the pain spasms are less frequent now but still intense when they happen. I have been staying in Superior with our daughter's family, Mary Lou and Don Griffith. I came home tonight to take care of mail and refill his portable oxygen tanks for the trip home. Will update Caring Bridge when he is home or if I have any other news.

Love to all, Karen

Friday, October 14, 2011 4:26 PM, CDT

Dan came home this afternoon. The two new medications helped the chest pain, and they reduced the pain from an 8 in a 1-10 ratio to 2 or 3, which we can handle with our home medication. He traveled well and is now asleep in the recliner. The new drugs are pretty powerful for chest and esophagus pain so, hopefully, we will be able to cut back on how often he takes them before too long. He is very tired and sleeps a lot since he started them. It will take some time for him to regain his strength after spending 4 days in bed. We are so happy to be home again. The Hospice team is on call tonight for us, and a nurse will be out here tomorrow to check him over. Thanks for the entire wonderful guest book comments, the emails, cards, and calls. We both appreciate them very much.

Sunday, October 16, 2011 2:11 PM, CDT

Visits from family and friends

Dan is doing OK, he still has spasms of pain, but sleeping well and now is eating without difficulties. He is on a soft diet. The pain medication makes him very sleepy. The hospice nurse was here and all his vitals were OK. We have had many calls from friends offering to help us in any way and we appreciate that very much. Thanks also for all the comments on this site, the emails, and cards.

I was reading through the entries I made on the journal and was sorry to see that I forgot to mention the wonderful visit we had with Dan's cousin, John and his wife, Janet Ahern. They live in Hudson, Wisconsin and were up to see us this summer. We were so happy to see them. John and Janet are also taking an active role in visiting and helping our 101 1/2 year old Aunt Verna in Sioux Falls and we are so thankful they are able to do that. John came out and spent time with us last Fall when we moved her out of her condo. She is in an assisted living and as soon as they heard she had a fall this summer they drove out to see her and updated us on her condition. It is difficult to stay in touch with cousins when we live so far apart but John and Janet have gone out of their way to stay in touch with us and we are very thankful for that. We have also received messages from his sisters, Ellen and Cathy throughout Dan's illness. Thank to everyone.

Tuesday, October 18, 2011 9:46 AM, CDT

I wish I could say Dan was feeling much better. The pain spasms continue off and on all day, average about a 4 from 1-10 ratio of pain. One pain med was increased yesterday afternoon, but still no change this morning. I woke up by a loud rattling from his lungs this morning at 4:45 so I set up his nebulizer treatment, which really helps. He did sleep in his recliner off and on for about two hours then. The only time he does not have the spasms is when he is sleeping which is good. Hope to have some more ideas this morning after the Hospice team meeting. The nurse will be out here again today. His oncologist left us a message yesterday thru his nurse that we need to contact the GI Doctor again and that some people have to remove the stent. We don't want that to happen, as he will be unable to eat normally so hope someone comes up with some other ideas on the chest pain. Please keep praying that his pain stops - we need your prayers.

Thursday, October 20, 2011 5:26 PM, CDT

Dan in Hospital again
I took Dan to the emergency room of St. Mary's in Duluth early

yesterday morning as he was having continuous horrible pain spasms in the middle of his chest. He was admitted to the Hospice Unit and is still there. I stayed in his room with him last night. The doctors are trying all new meds to stop these spasms and they have the pain down from horrible to medium but this morning he was still having four attacks per hour. Before I left at 2:30 PM, they were coming a little less frequent. On Wednesday, they tried four new meds; today they increased the dosage on two of them. If this does not work, tomorrow, they will try different ones. The head GI Doc who did this will be out of town until Monday, but his PA was in today and another partner of his have been in conference with the Doctor who is the Hospice Director. The Oncologist is also part of this discussion and the big question is - Did the GI Doctor see a mass (or tumor) that is separated from the esophagus or could it have been an enlarged esophagus. His notes and photos all show an enlargement outside of the esophagus, however, the CT scan done of the chest a few days before does not back this up so they all want to be in agreement on it. He told us after the stent procedure that this mass was pressing on it and closed up the esophagus, and that within another week, there would have been no opening for food. If it is a separate mass, they told us it is probably cancerous, and they can direct radiation to it, shrink it, and hopefully, stop the pain. It may still be pressing on the esophagus causing these pain spasms. The procedures will be decided on Monday as they want to continue to try to stop the pain without another invasive procedure, if possible, and the Doctor who did the stent will be back in town for a decision on Monday. Their goal is to continue to sedate him for the pain. In that he is sleeping without pain, they are trying to sedate him so he can be totally relaxed as much as possible without putting him to sleep in hopes the pain will stop while he is awake too.

I am home tonight to pick up some things we forgot in our rush out of here yesterday, most importantly, our cell phone and Nook chargers, along with some personal items for Dan. I will be returning to the hospital early tomorrow morning.

We are very impressed with the Hospice unit—he has a private room with a flat screen TV, a chair that rolls out for a bed for me, and the staff is outstanding. All of them treat us like family, so Dan is as comfortable as he can be right now with this continuous pain. Thank you for the prayers, he sure needs them now. We are receiving great support from the Hospital Chaplain (he brought us the Eucharist last night), the Hospice Chaplain, our Home Hospice Nurse, the Social Worker, and the Bereavement Counselor. They have all visited and comforted both of this through another stay in the hospital. They, and all the dedicated nursing staff and doctors are truly angels sent to us by the Lord. Our daughter, Mary Lou, is right by our side meeting with the staff to ease things for us, and our son, Pat and his wife Tambrey, have been in several times also the last two days. The other family members are in touch with us several times a day by phone and are ready to drive up here if we need them.

Of course, Dan, as usual, is more worried about the family then himself. He says continually that he does not want to put us through all this and we continue to remind him that it is not his choice to be suffering like this, and that we all want to be by his side for whatever happens, and that we all love him very much.

Friday, October 21, 2011 5:48 PM, CDT

Home again

Dan came home this afternoon from the hospital. The pain spasms are less frequent and less intense. The pain episodes started changing yesterday afternoon. He is still experiencing some spasms but he said they are too mild (2 out of 10) to even mention. We have several new drugs and they have certainly helped. Dan told me to write that the Power of Prayer is the best medicine he has received and we thank all of you for these prayers.

Our son, Dan, is on his way up here from Appleton to help this weekend as he expects his dad to be very weak after spending a great deal of time in bed the past two weeks. He spent 8 days in the hospital during that time. His body is also adjusting to these new drugs and that takes a toll also. Will update the site when something new to report. God Bless you all for your prayers, emails, cards and comments on this site and our Facebook wall.

Sunday, October 30, 2011 5:49 AM, CDT

I am sorry to say that Dan is not doing well. He is awake about four hours a day now. All our children are taking turns being here now and we are trying hard to keep him comfortable.

Wednesday, November 2, 2011 11:39 AM, CDT

Dan is doing better now. He is awake more and we were happy to go to Mass on Tuesday. His breathing is not good, however, the pain spasms are almost gone. He is still having some chest pains, but he says they are different now and the nitro paste treatments are working to relieve the pain (along with 14 other medicines). The support, comfort and help from all our family has been out-standing- they have been here with us for two weeks, taking turns so we were not alone and doing everything from caring for him to cooking, cleaning and outdoor stuff. All their loving care has helped to give him more strength and we are so thankful to them for their time as we know how busy their lives are with work and children. They tell Dan that spending time with him is where they want to be right now when he starts feeling guilty for the time they spend with us helping out. Dan said today to our son, Danny, as he was leaving for Appleton that, "Words cannot express how much I appreciate what you and all your brothers and sister are doing for me."

Dan also enjoyed visits from his two sisters, Peg Likar and Pat Bies, with their families this past week. We see Dr. Lalich, the On-cologist, next Tuesday and will update this site after that visit.

We believe that the power of prayer is also helping him very much—thanks to all of you for these prayers. "Even though we walk in the shadow of death, we shall fear no evil, for He is at our side with His rod and His staff. He gives us courage! The Lord is our Shepherd."

Tuesday, November 8, 2011 7:52 PM, CST

Dan had an appointment today with Dr. Lalich, our Oncologist. The doctor did not hear any fluids in his lungs, which is a good thing. He told us the difficulty with thick secretions, the chest pain, and increased breathing difficulties he experiences every day are all

the natural progression of the lung cancer. The cancer has spread to his esophagus, which we learned last month when Dan was still in the hospital. He still has chest pain but the pains are not as frequent, nor as severe, as they were when he was in the hospital. The doctor said the lung cancer is advancing. He is able to eat a soft diet now and food tastes better since he had the stent procedure.

Ten days ago, our Hospice Nurse told me that he probably has about two weeks left to live because of the noise in the lungs, and he was sleeping all day long, awake only to eat and take medication. Today the doctor said that we should expect that pattern to continue (some good days and some bad days) until he eventually will not have any strength and will have to stay in bed and will sleep almost all day and night. He told us that he will have no pain and sleeping is not a bad thing at that point in time.

Only the Lord knows when this will happen and until then, Dan will continue to fight the battle with all of his loving family by his side. His attitude and courage is amazing. He is ready for whatever happens next. Dan is a wonderful husband, father, grandfather, brother, cousin, nephew, brother-in-law and uncle who loves his family and believes that The Lord Jesus is at his side and will take him home when the time is right. Our goal is to love him and make him as comfortable as possible with little or no pain during this time.

Thanks to everyone for the emails, cards and prayers. We appreciate your love and support during this past year. His next goal is to live to November 19th, which is one year since he was diagnosed with lung cancer. I will update this site whenever there is more news to share.

Wednesday, November 9, 2011 7:09 PM, CST

Thoughts from Dan

I truly feel in my heart I am ready to meet my Lord and Master. I have a loving family and I'm not ready to leave them, but if it's God's will, so be it! If we do His will, we will be spending eternity with Him. Billy Graham was once asked if he was worried about dying. His response was, "I am not worried about dying, I am just worried about the process." I think that is how most of us feel - we don't want to die with a lot of pain and agony, we just want to go as peacefully as possible. That is the reason I want to spend my final days at home where I am with my loving and caring family. Love, Dan

Friday, November 11, 2011 2:56 PM, CST

In Honor of all Veterans

Happy Veteran's Day, to my love! Dan served in the Army from 1954-1962. He was attached to the 11th Airborne stationed in Augsburg, Germany. He was in the Scout Dog Platoon, training dogs to search and find the enemy. His dog's name was Nero.

Sunday, November 20, 2011 12:43 PM, CST

A quick update: Dan's health is declining some every day now. Breathing is very bad, he is sleeping quite a bit now, and when awake we have to use a transfer belt to help him walk, as he is very weak. We find it is easier for him to eat at his recliner instead of trying to walk to the table, as he can't breathe when he gets there. He still has a great sense of humor and never complains. He has some pain, but he says it is infrequent and not too bad.

If you want to call and talk to him, he usually sleeps right after lunch until about 4 PM every day now. Mid mornings (after 10) are best for calling him. Our children and their spouses are here often now and a great help and loving support. We have also had visits and help from our grandchildren, which we also appreciate very much. To answer the questions we have received in calls and emails about the identity of the main photo on our site, it is Jesus Christ, as painted by an eight year old girl, Akiane Kramarik, who had visions of heaven, talked with the Lord, and became a famous painter. After she did this painting, the young boy in the book "Heaven is for Real", told his family, "This is a painting of Jesus and I was with Him". He died on an operating table and spent ten minutes in heaven. A great book to read. We want to wish all of you a Happy Thanksgiving. Hug your spouse and your kids for us! We thank you for your continued prayers.

Tuesday, November 22, 2011 1:05 PM, CST

Dad passed away today, quietly, at home, at 9:30 a.m. this morning.

Daniel E Collins: May 30, 1934 — November 22, 2011.

We are lucky and thankful to have a father that has been a wonderful role model. A father to be proud of. A Memorial Mass will be held at 11:00 am on Friday, November 25, 2011 at St. Michael's Church, Iron River, WI. Visitation will begin at 10:00 a.m.

Pat Collins, Dan Collins, Joe Collins and Mary Lou Griffith.

Wednesday, November 23, 2011 11:02 AM, CST

OBITUARY

Daniel E. Collins, 77, of Iron River, passed away Tuesday, Nov. 22, 2011, in his home.

Dan was born May 30, 1934, in Saint Paul, the son of Daniel C. and Vivian (Ahern) Collins. He attended Saint Mary's of the Lake Grade School in White Bear Lake, Minn. He then attended Cretin High School in Saint Paul and graduated in 1953, after which he attended Saint Thomas College in Saint Paul.

He was a U.S. Army Veteran serving in Germany as a dog handler and cook from 1954 to 1962. On Sept 9, 1961, he was united in marriage to Karen M. Peterson in Superior. He owned and operated the Country Closet in Iron River as well as being a handyman and cabin caretaker. He also worked at Tester Corporation and Brule Corporation, before which he was the manager of the Holiday Station Store, Kroger Foods and Warner Hardware.

He enjoyed reading, traveling, general handyman jobs, boating, camping with family, cooking and spending time with his wife, Karen, and his children and grandchildren.

He was a member of Saint Michael's Catholic Church in Iron River, where he was a prayer leader, lector and Eucharistic Minister. He was also a member of the Knights of Columbus, the Iron River Foundation, the Iron River Lakes Association, the Lions Club, the American Legion and the Iron River Chamber of Commerce.

Dan is survived by his wife of 50-years, Karen, of Iron River; children Daniel M. (Ann) of Appleton, WI. Patrick T. (Tambrey) of Duluth, Joseph V. (Colleen) of Two Rivers, Wis., and Mary Lou T. (Donald) Griffith of Superior; grandchildren Nathan Collins, Michelle Collins, Brennen Collins, Reid Collins, Paige Collins, Chase Collins, Logan Griffith, and Kalen Griffith; sisters Patricia (Richard) Bies of Breezy Point, Minn., Margaret (Peg) Likar of Duluth, and Jeanne (Donald) McNeally of Vadnais Heights, Minn.; aunt Verna Ahern Shreves of Sioux Falls, S.D.; and several nieces, nephews and cousins.

A GATHERING OF FAMILY AND FRIENDS: 10 until the 11 a.m. memorial Mass Friday, Nov. 25, in Saint Michael's Catholic Church in Iron River with Father Michael Crisp as celebrant. Interment will take place at Saint Michael Cemetery, Iron River.

Funeral arrangements have been entrusted to the Mountain Funeral Home and Cremation Services of Ashland and Mellen, Wis.

Saturday, November 26, 2011 9:24 AM, CST

Grief is a journey of the heart to be taken one step at a time side-by-side with the Lord. Blessed are those who mourn, for they shall be comforted. Matthew 5:4

Thank you for walking the journey with Dan and I and our children and grandchildren. We will never forget all the wonderful messages and prayers. Dan read them all and enjoyed them very much, as well as all the rest of our family.

We had over 150 families and friends attend his funeral Mass yesterday and I have posted four photos for you that were taken by our son, Dan.

Our gratitude and love to all of you
from all of our Collins family.

Thursday, December 1, 2011 11:02 AM, CST

A call from Heaven

On Monday morning following Dan's funeral, I placed a call to the Veteran's Administration for insurance purposes. I was placed on hold twice and while I was holding, a song started to play. *DANNY BOY* was the song. Mary Lou, our daughter, was with me and I asked her to listen to confirm that was really what was happening. She agreed with me and the entire song was played before a lady came on the line. By then, I was crying and I asked her if she knew the title of the music playing and she told me they did not know. I told her "I am calling to inform you my Danny Boy, my husband, has died, and you played *Danny Boy* *for me, which was his favorite song and it was sung at our Anniversary Mass and at his Funeral Mass by our son, Joe.* After I calmed down, she took his name and information and then said, "I have something else to tell you before you go." She then said, "I want you to know that I have a brother-in-law named Daniel Collins."

Dan and I had talked about heaven and we both agreed that whoever got there first would do everything possible to let the other one know they were in Heaven and doing fine. I received my call from Heaven.

Thank you, Dan and the Lord God.

Sunday, December 4, 2011 11:16 AM, CST

This is my reply to all the cards, letters and emails I have received from you wondering how I am doing: A new journey began for me on November 22, 2011. A journey to live without my soul mate of 50-plus years. A person cannot practice for this role. Dan's sister, Peg (who is also a widow), told me that we should write a book about how to be a widow. It is a role we do not wish for in our life. Sometimes I feel I was cut in half, with the best half gone to heaven. The Lord has blessed us with four great caring children, spouses, and eight grandchildren who will fill my life with caring love. He was also holding my hand this past year and will until He calls me home.

I am blessed to live in a small town of Iron River where people show they care for each other. I go to Mass, with hugs on the way in and the way out, in the bank. the grocery store, and even the post office. "How are you doing, Karen?" All I can say is, I'm doing OK–that is exactly what Dan said the past year, every time anyone (including me) asked him that question. How can I say anything different after watching his courage daily for a year?

Today started with 2-3 inches of snow and while I was shoveling the sidewalk, my neighbor Barb, who suffered the death of her daughter and spouse in the same year, was on her John Deere tractor, and was blowing away all the snow in my driveway. How can I NOT be OK with friends like that in my life? Yes, I am staying in our home in Iron River this winter, with many family visits.

The Lord is the Leader in my new journey of life. When the Lord called Dan home, Dan replied, "So be it." He wrote this to all of you on caring bridge a few days before he died. I will now follow his great example to the best of my ability, to take on this unwanted title of widow, and follow the Lord's future plans for me. I also say, "So be it!"

Thank you for all your emails, cards and prayers. We will always remember the love and comfort you gave to our family.

Love, Karen

DAN'S FINAL MOMENTS ON EARTH – NOVEMBER 22, 2011

Dan woke up this morning with a deep cough, which was something new. He walked to the living room with very little help to sit in his recliner, which looked out over Buskey Bay. Shortly after joking about the menu for breakfast with his son, Joe, he started to eat scrambled eggs.

Within minutes, he started having trouble swallowing the food and Joe took his tray away. He began to gasp for air, so Joe changed him back to the oxygen mask (which he used while sleeping), with hope the change may help him breathe. Dan continued struggling for air so it was obvious the oxygen was not helping at all. As all this was happening, Joe noticed four geese land on the bay in front of our window. I was kneeling in front of Dan's chair and he was holding my hand tightly. Joe was also kneeling at his side, and Dan was holding his hand tightly too.

Joe knew then that his Dad was dying, he put down his hand and moved behind the chair and began to gently massage his dad's shoulders, bending to whisper in his ear softly, "Don't fight it any more, Dad." As Dan held my hand tightly, I said softly and repeatedly, "Precious Lord, please take him home, Precious Lord, please take him home." Dan's eyes were locked on the window and he

raised his right hand up and took his last breath at 9:30 a. m. Joe
looked out at the lake and the geese were flying away.

> The Precious Lord came to take him home.
> HE gave Dan wings and then the honor guard of four geese
> escorted their wounded friend straight up to Heaven.

Here is a copy of the email sent from our son, Joe, when I asked
him to read my accounting of Dan's last day on earth before it was
published:

Mom:
I think you have done a wonderful job of capturing that moment.
I have told people that there have been few moments in life
where the memory will be forever etched in my mind. The births of
my children and being with you and Dad as he went to meet Jesus
are those I will never forget. I give thanks to God I was present when
these events occurred.
My friend/instructor from the FBI that I work with is now retired
and a minister in DC. He explained that when your loved one is alive
you are able to spend some time with them. When they pass away
they are with you always.
Love you – Joe

REFLECTION

Why did the geese land on our Bay that morning on that day?

To quote my publisher (and my friend), "Animals have a connection with God and the afterlife that we don't share." So I did some research and this article seemed to satisfy my question:

Scientists say that, "When a goose gets sick or is wounded by gunshot, and falls out of the formation, two other geese fall out with that goose and follow it down to lend help and protection. They stay with the fallen goose until it is able to fly or until it dies; and only then do they launch out on their own, or fly with another formation to catch up with their own flock."

All through Dan's life, he stood faithfully with his family, his friends and his neighbors when they were wounded (hurt, sick, or lonely). He was always ready and willing to pray for them, to visit the sick and homebound, bringing the Eucharist for nourishment of their soul, and to comfort the lonely. Sometimes, it was simply driving an elderly man who lived alone into town for coffee and breakfast every morning for several years. Other times, it was when he dropped everything and drove to South Dakota to help his 100-year-old Aunt who lived alone and called for help. Dan would also stay with these folks until they were ready to fly on their own.

Now it was his turn. The geese were there to be at his side protecting him when he was wounded and unable to fly. After Dan received his wings from the Lord, they proudly escorted him to life everlasting, in their usual formation.

KAREN'S STORY

How do you describe a faithful Man?

Before starting my story, I decided to do some research about different kinds of men and I came across many stories about ordinary men. I found one that was very appropriate for my story, which is from the *Christian Blog for Everyone*.

"Jesus was an *ordinary man*. He was not perfect. He was not perfect in a sense that he can falter. When He was born, He cannot talk, He cannot walk, He cannot count. He cannot read.

He was not perfect because He cannot speak English nor French, His mother has to feed Him, He was taught how to walk, eat etc. Jesus was an *ordinary man*. Everything He did can be done by anyone. He was not a superman.

Jesus was an *ordinary man*. He was ordinary because it is the essence of Incarnation. To be a real man, an ordinary man, not a superman, *so* that *we can know* how to live as an *ordinary man or woman* in conformity to *what God wanted us to be.* Jesus is like anyone of us, except sin. Yes, except sin, because while we are sinners, it is possible that one can live without sinning."

Another ordinary man

Dan always thought he was an *ordinary man*, nothing special, and by no means a superman. He held many jobs. Paper boy, golf caddy, dog trainer in the U.S, Army, laborer in a cold storage plant and in later years, a retail store manager, sole proprietor of a clothing store, and finally a handyman with electrical, plumbing, painting, and carpentry skills. A friend called him her Wisconsin husband. Whenever she and her husband had a problem at their cabin, they called Dan and he was there to fix it immediately.

Not a perfect man

Dan had his faults like any *ordinary man*. He was born the youngest and only son of a loving Christian family with three sisters. He shared his memories with me of early struggles in a Catholic grade school where his parents forced him to stay an extra year because he had difficulty with concentration. He received a passing grade so he earned advancement to the next grade, but because he had difficulties in concentration, his parents and the Nun decided it was better for him to be held back a year. His friends went on and it hurt him deeply, something he sadly remembered the rest of his life.

A Man of abiding faith

Dan was a man who loved God with all his heart and soul and he tried hard to share his faith with his four children. He did this by good example and by teaching them a sense of right and wrong, which was instilled in him as a child. His father was a loving man, but did not spare the rod to spoil the child. Dan saw his share of spankings and he told me proudly, with a twinkle in his eye, that he usually earned them all. Our greatest family times together were taking camping trips, even when they were a short drive from home. All we needed to be happy was to be together on a lake, river or the woods. Dan was depressed when he had to tell us we were unable to go camping because he had to work. Every Sunday we attended church services as a family and when we were camping, Dan sometimes drove miles to find a church. In his mind, there was never a good reason to miss Mass on Sunday, unless you went on Saturday. On one of those trips, our son, Pat's friend, Bill Penning, came with us and he didn't regularly attend our church. By mistake, he was suddenly in line to receive Communion. He was very nervous, trying hard to watch others ahead of him, so he'd do the right thing. Evidently, the Priest had been watching Bill's behavior, looking at everyone receiving communion, thinking it was not the usual behavior of a devout boy preparing to receive Communion. Recently, Bill came to visit Dan and reminded him of this incident, He told Dan that when he got to the front of the church, the Priest embarrassed him saying aloud with a stern voice, "Fold your hands and look reverent." Bill said, "I can laugh about it now, but I always remember how much I appreciated that you jumped right to my defense, publicly in Mass, which probably was pretty tough for a man as religious as you." As soon as Dan realized what was happening to Bill, he walked ahead of the line to stand right next to Bill and said to the Priest, "He is new at this Father, so let's be patient with him." The Priest smiled then and Bill, after receiving his First Communion in our church, made a quick retreat back to the pew.

After Dan's bout with rectal caner in 1984, he started attending daily Mass besides the regular weekend Mass. He told me he was on "borrowed time" and the least he could do was to go and thank God for giving him additional time with his family.

In later years, Dan became an avid reader, He finished a forty book series based on an inspirational family saga last winter, and he read his bible daily. He went to sleep every night with his rosary, (made in Ireland) in his hands, a gift from his son and daughter-in-law, Dan and Ann.

We shared many discussions about life, death and afterlife. We promised each other that whichever one of us arrived in heaven first, we would do everything possible to let the other one know they were there and doing fine. He told me he did not understand how any person was able to endure a terminal illness without believing in God and life everlasting. He showed no fear of death after he was told he had less than a year to live, because of his abiding faith and love of God. He knew where he was going next and that confidence gave him comfort and peace. He was sad for those without faith, especially during their final years on earth.

A generous man

Dan served many volunteer positions both in our church and in the community. He shared his time with those less fortunate by serving meals at community centers. He grew up in the depression era and watched carefully how we spent our money. At one time when he was a salesman on the road, he received a daily travel allowance. He stayed at cheap motels and used the money he saved to buy groceries. Every time he returned home, he brought several bags of groceries, and it made me wonder if he had spent any money to eat on these trips.

A man who showed love for his family

Dan was a chain smoker since high school, but he quit smoking immediately one day in 1974 after a telephone call home. I had taken the three youngest children to the Doctor that morning as they had been suffering a long time with coughs. The diagnosis was that all three of our children were allergic to smoke and were suffering from the cigarette smoke he created in our home. Once Dan heard that message, he never smoked another cigarette in his life. He had one left in his pocket and planned to go to the store after the call to buy another pack of cigarettes. Before this, he had tried several times to stop smoking and failed. Once he heard from the doctor that he was causing the illness his children suffered, he quit immediately. He was able to tell you the exact day and hour he quit smoking.

Dan was a loving father to a daughter, Mary Lou, and three sons, Daniel, Patrick and Joseph. He was grandfather to eight, Nathan, Michelle, Brennen, Reid, Paige, Chase, Logan and Kalen. He loved to be with them and attended their concerts and sports whenever possible. He loved it when they came to the lake where he pulled them on tubes behind our pontoon, watched them swim and sometimes joined them playing cards and dominos. He took his last kayak ride, with a big smile on his face, last September with his oldest grandson, Nathan.

In 1979, our family made a decision to move to Northern Wisconsin, which is my former home and where one of our favorite camping sites was located on land that we inherited from my parents. Our oldest son, Danny, was going to begin his senior year in high school that year. Dan wanted to make the move but decided we should delay the move for another year so Danny could graduate with his friends. He didn't want Danny to suffer in life by being pulled out of school before graduation, like he had been years ago in grade school. Danny made it loud and clear that he wanted to move to Iron River before his senior year, so Dan agreed to quit a good paying job and move to a small town in Wisconsin. It was a hard decision for him to make. We moved from a large 4-bedroom home in the city into a mobile home in the woods, without water or sewer, and we did it before selling our city home. At the first parent teacher conference in their new school, every one of the teachers told us that our four kids came to school with a sparkle in their eyes and were doing very well in their studies.

A man who endured suffering and instilled faith in his children

In 1980, a family snowmobile/car accident devastated Dan when two of our children were injured by his car as he and our son Danny were driving home from work and met two of our children (Mary Lou and Pat) driving our snowmobile on a blind corner on a narrow snow covered road. As he turned the corner, they were in the middle of the road, and he was unable to stop as they were coming straight at the car. He hit the brake and swerved, so it was not a head on collision, but they were both thrown off the machine into a snow bank and lay there crying with broken and injured legs. When we arrived in the emergency room with the whole family, the Doctor came in with the x-rays in his hands and I heard him ask the nurse, "Where are the two kids with broken legs?" Then he heard voices and saw them lying on stretchers and repeating prayers with us, never stopping. The doctor was amazed as the x-rays, Pat and Mary Lou had broke the same leg, both the femur and tibia bones and Mary Lou had severe skin damage to her leg. He said these kids should be screaming in pain, as he gave them pain injections. Days later, a man who was in that ambulance, came up to me to tell me he will always remember how we all prayed during the trip to the hospital. It took years for Dan to stop dreaming about the accident and for the children to convince him that they did not blame him for the accident. Tears filled his eyes from then on anytime some-one discussed the accident. Shortly after the accident, Dan started to suffer with severe episodes of back pain. He continued to suffer with the pain until it disappeared, after he was prescribed morphine for his lung cancer in 2010. One doctor suggested it might have been a result of that accident. We all knew the accident had broken his heart.

The abiding faith of a dying man

It is extremely hard for any man to give up his independence, especially with his personal needs. The biggest obstacle we faced in the last month of his life was to get him to agree to accept my help in taking care of his colostomy, which was a result of his rectal cancer in 1984. When I saw that he was unable to do it any longer, I had to beg him to let me take care of it for him. We cried together then and he reluctantly agreed. I was so thankful as he told me, "That went a lot better than I ever expected." As he grew weaker, he let the children and I care for him and he was always saying, "Thank you." Hospice offered him a personal aide, but he didn't really want a stranger to do these things for him, especially, when he had his family by his side, ready to do anything to make him comfortable. He never complained about his cancer and he often expressed that he had no fear of dying. A few weeks before he died, he was having breathing difficulties and we cried together. He said to me, "When is enough, enough? I am ready for it to be over." My answer was, "When the Lord is ready to take you home, Dan." He told me that he agreed with that statement and he did not refer to his suffering again.

A man with a sense of humor he shared with his family

He made us laugh over the years telling hundreds of jokes, remembering every line. His youngest grandson, Logan, called him, The Riddle Grandpa, as he would go on repeating long funny stories to him and his sister, Kalen. One of his favorite stories was, "Why is a FIRE Engine RED in color?"

Answer: FIRE Engine has LADDER. LADDER has STEPS. STEPS are to be climbed on FOOT. FOOT is measured by a RULER. RULER can be a KING or QUEEN. ELIZABETH is the QUEEN of ENGLAND. ELIZABETH is also the name of a SHIP. SHIP sails on WATER. WATER has FISHES. FISHES have FINS. The people of FINLAND are called FINS. The national FLAG of FINLAND is RED. So that is why a FIRE Engine is RED in color.

He brought us all to laughter so hard that our stomachs hurt with his jokes, stories and what we call his one liners, which was usually a crazy pun following something we did or said. He had a beautiful tenor voice and would sing silly songs while we traveled across the country on camping trips. We soon joined him in the songs and the miles would disappear. His humor was a blessing for our family and a legacy that his children and grandchildren share today, with their one line jokes and funny stories they learned from their dad. On the last day of his life, he shared that wit with Joe and I, minutes before he died.

He loved most animals, however, there were two that he did not welcome in our yard. First came the squirrels that ate all the bird-seed from his feeders almost as soon as he put it out. It was a daily battle trying to beat them at their game, but he lost the battle most of the time, laughing at their antics. The second problem was the geese that pooped big time in our front yard every time they swam ashore. He thought they were beautiful birds, and loved to watch the goslings. Because of them, we purchased an old-fashioned bike horn that has a rubber ball to squeeze that emits a loud horn noise. Dan used it to chase the geese out of the yard as soon as they came ashore. However, he refused to scare them when they had their little goslings in the yard.

The geese came to be with him during the last days of his life in more ways than one. He needed medicine immediately when he woke up to help him breathe and before he was able to walk into the living room. We had to figure out a way for him to alert me that he was awake because I was usually up much earlier. He couldn't blow a whistle or holler because of his difficulty breathing. I finally remembered the horn we used for the geese and brought it into the bedroom one morning telling him I had a brainstorm. He had to squeeze the horn as soon as he woke up and I would be at this side. He laughed to hear the geese were finally going to help him out, he was a bit reluctant to use it, but I made him promise, and he was a man who kept his word. The geese horn went off every morning in our bedroom. I ran in quickly with his medicine and nebulizer treatment to help him breathe and it worked great.

A humble man

I heard the words, "It humbles me," from Dan many times during the past year. It humbled him from the day he was diagnosed with Lung Cancer that his children were always by his side. One of the four of them was always with us at treatments and doctor appointments. They left their home and jobs continuously to be with him during the past year. Their spouses and our grandchildren also came as often as possible to be at his side. Dan enjoyed the times he shared with them very much, but also expressed that he felt guilty because of the time they were spending away from their homes and jobs. They told him, repeatedly, that they were with him because that is where they needed to be. Nathan, our eldest grandson from Appleton, was invited to live with his Aunt Mary Lou's family to attend nursing college during this time, and he also visited often, willing to help anyway possible. Dan was humbled by all their help, and by the calls, visits, cards, emails, and the messages on CaringBridge, and by the special gifts he received from his grandchildren and friends.

Until we meet again, my loving husband

Dan was 27 and I was 19 when we married in 1961. His parish priest told his Mom, "Their marriage will never last as he is too old for her." He went on to say, "Karen will want to go out dancing while Dan will want to sit home and that will bring trouble to their marriage." We laughed about that story many times over the years while we were dancing the jitterbug and we wished the priest was alive to invite him to our 50th wedding anniversary.

Dan told me he will never say good-by to me, but he told me, "I will say, '*Until We Meet Again.*'"

He was my true love, my better half, and was the only person to call me *Michula*, an Irish / Gallic word for My Love. One night shortly after he died, I was crying in bed, unable to sleep, and I heard him calling out to me, *Michula, Michula, Michula.* I knew then "he was still with me," and I went to sleep.

Soon after, I found a small newspaper ad on his dresser tray that he had cut out and saved, folded in small pieces. Much to my surprise, Dan had chosen a gift for me to wear after he died. It was an elegant teardrop pendant crafted in sterling silver with a sparkling diamond, surrounded by an exquisitely created opal (my birthstone) reflecting the colorful splendor of dawn. The back of the pendant is lovingly engraved with: "I am with you still in each new dawn." I ordered that pendant for my last Christmas gift, and I know he wanted me to wear it, and remember that, "He is with me still."

Dan, an *ordinary man*, trying all his life to follow the example set by *Jesus*, his Savior and Redeemer,

An ordinary man.

To his family, he was an extra-ordinary man.

Danny Boy.

And we loved him so............

I Am With You Still

I give you this one thought to keep
I am with you still – do not weep.

I am a thousand winds that blow.
I am the diamond glints on the snow.
I am the sunlight on ripened grain.
I am the gentle autumn's rain.
When you awaken in the morning's hush,
I am the swift uplifting rush
Of quiet birds in circled flight.
I am the soft stars that shine at night.

Do not think of me as gone –
I am with you still –
In each new dawn.

(This poem arrived with the pendant Dan chose for me)

EPILOGUE

I read a new message on Caring Bridge shortly after Dan's funeral and this message stated that Dan's faith and courage continually inspired them and the whole community. Their comment was repeated in other telephone calls, cards and emails we received all year.

I began to wonder if reading about Dan's life this past year might inspire other families going through terminal illness or personal struggles in their life. Is it possible his story might help others to reach out for the Lord's Hand for strength in their suffering?

How does an ordinary man face a diagnosis of terminal lung cancer with a maximum life expectancy of one year? How is he able to face it without fear, instead with courage and faith? I hope Danny Boy will show the reader how one man, an ordinary person, with faith and trust in the Lord was able to die, without fear, but instead with dignity and peace.

The Lord led me to share Dan's story and then he also led me to Mike Savage, my publisher, who coached me with patience and understanding, a man who believes in the Holy Spirit.

"THY will be done on earth as it is in heaven."

GUEST BOOK

Friday, November 19, 2010 9:04 PM

You can be assured Karen and Dan, that you are not alone on this journey! Our prayers and thoughts, and the prayers and thoughts of so many other people who care about you are with you also. Remember The Footprints Story? Oh, my gosh!!!! I just saw the footprints on this page after I typed that! It gave me a chill! The Lord assures the man with the words, "My precious child, I love you and would never forsake you. During those times of trial and suffering, when you could see only one set of footprints, it was then I carried you."

With love and prayers, Julie & Jerry Peck

Saturday, November 20, 2010 12:23 AM

My sister speaks words all of us are feeling now for Dan and you, Karen. You aren't alone in this. We are all here for you now. Distance may separate us, but prayers will keep you close to my heart. I pray your strong faith and family will bring peace to your days as you travel on this new journey.

Sending love, Karen Daniels

Saturday, November 20, 2010 6:52 AM

Dear Dan & Karen:

So sorry to hear of your diagnosis. Jim and I will be thinking of you and praying that the chemo will slow down the cancer. Jim's sister is currently undergoing chemo for lung cancer also. This is her second round, the first time she was in remission for two years. So it does work! Keep a positive attitude and know many are thinking of you.

Charlotte & Jim Selgeby

Saturday, November 20, 2010 8:25 AM

What can we say! Our love and prayers will be with you on this journey. You are two of the best people we know. Let us know if

there's <u>anything</u> that we can do. God be with you.
  Tom and Ellen Hoeltgen

Saturday, November 20, 2010 9:05 AM

  Well I see that you're still up in the Superior Wisconsin area. I am still in Ontario, Wisconsin area. I still come down to the Bank everyday. I am enjoying my retirement and do some traveling. I still remember that you had stopped by some time ago. I will be going to Mass today to sing. He who sings prays twice. So I'll sing twice as hard today but it won't sound any better. Talk at you later.
  Richard DelMedico

Saturday, November 20, 2010 9:14 AM

You are in my thoughts and prayers.
Colleen Collins

Saturday, November 20, 2010 9:33 AM

  Hey Mr. and Mrs. Collins! Kathy and I are thinking of you and praying for God's Will to be done. Here's to your comfort and peace today and always!
  And keep Joe away from the TV today. He's not going to be happy during the MI/WI game :-)
  Perry Kingsbury

Saturday, November 20, 2010 9:57 AM

  Dear Karen and Dan:
  We are so sad to hear about your diagnosis Dan. We know your faith is strong and you have beat cancer before. We are thinking and praying for you and know you are not walking alone. The treatment will be tiring, but you are a tough guy. If you need anything we are here.
  Love, John and Jeanne Joseph

Saturday, November 20, 2010 10:35 AM

Praying for you everyday Grandma and Grandpa. Be strong and have faith.

Love, Paige Collins

Saturday, November 20, 2010 10:54 AM

God's love to you Dan and your family. He does work miracles and will be with you as you go through your treatments. Know that we will have you in our prayers.

Our love, Jerry & Judy Darwin

Saturday, November 20, 2010 12:32 PM

You are loved, Dan, by a huge circle of family & friends who hope and pray will provide both you and Karen comfort and strength on your journey to fight this disease once again! And be assured that I will continue "storming the heavens with prayers" as Mom always said in hours of great need! **God** IS listening to all our prayers!

Love, Mary Peterson

Saturday, November 20, 2010 2:02 PM

Dan and Karen:

I was so sorry to hear this news. After reading your story I can see you are a person of great strength, with a very loving and supportive family. You are in my thoughts.

Mary Shreves, Willow, Alaska

Saturday, November 20, 2010 2:12 PM

Dan, Karen and Family:

My prayers will be with you everyday. I have experienced the power of prayer so many times this past 3 months, so I know how powerful they can be. To have your family and so many friends with you is such a blessing. I am sure you will put up a good fight and win this battle. Miracles do happen.

Karen Wicklund

Saturday, November 20, 2010 2:38 PM

Uncle Dan and Aunt Karen:
You have been in our thoughts and prayers since Mom informed me of your diagnosis. Midori, Sakura, and I will be in Duluth for Christmas and we are looking forward to seeing you then. The Lord will provide you comfort and I know your faith will help you through this.
Love to both of you! Mike Likar

Saturday, November 20, 2010 3:33 PM

Dear Collins Family:
We are sorry to hear the news of your loved one, Daniel. We will pray for the strength for him to fight this and safe travels for all of you during the winter months as you begin this journey. Dan and Ann if there is anything we can do here in Darboy for you, please let us know...anything, anytime.
God's Blessings to all of you,
Matt & Amy Storm

Saturday, November 20, 2010 3:52 PM

Dear Dan & Karen
Our thoughts and prayers are with you. Dan looked so great when we saw you both in July...just can't believe how this could happen so fast. We enjoyed our time with you and hope we can come and see you again this summer. Wishing you strength to overcome this difficult treatment period. Please let us know if we can help in anyway.
Hugs from us all,
Jen, Mike and Caleigh Nystrom

Saturday, November 20, 2010 6:38 PM

Dan & Karen:
My thoughts and prayers are with you.
Tom Dooher

Saturday, November 20, 2010 6:41 PM

Greetings: Prayers and best wishes to the Collins family.
Gary V, CDH-'53
Gary Vadnais

Saturday, November 20, 2010 7:50 PM

Dear Karen and Dan:
What a shock to get your message today! Please know that we
are thinking of you both and holding you in our prayers as you set
forth on this journey. We love you both and know that the Lord will
give you many graces to sustain you and your family. Please let us
know at anytime if we can be of help in any way. We are just a phone
call away.
Love and prayers, Sue and John McLennan

Saturday, November 20, 2010 8:39 PM

Hello Mr. and Mrs. Collins:
We are sending you warm wishes and many prayers for healing,
strength and courage. Just know that you are not alone in this journey...you are surrounded by the strength of your amazing family
and friends near and far.
Much love from Amy and Dan Foster
(Joe and Colleen's friends from Neenah)

Saturday, November 20, 2010 9:06 P

Dan and Karen:
I remember you well from our days in 113 at Cretin. You are in
our prayers; best wishes and energy to you and your family.
Jim Farrell

Sunday, November 21, 2010 12:39 AM

Dan & Karen:
We were sad to hear of your cancer diagnoses. We both
know what a challenging situation that can be. It is good to hear you
are choosing to fight it. You will be in our thoughts & prayers.
Greg & Chris Ogren

Sunday, November 21, 2010 9:48 AM

Love you Grandpa
Chase Collins

Sunday, November 21, 2010 2:46 PM

DAN, YOU ARE ONE TOUGH SON-OF-A-GUN,AND WILL CON-
QUER THIS LATEST HEALTH PROBLEM. REMEMBER YOU ARE A
BROTHERS BOY. SAINT JOHN BAPTIST-PRAY FOR US- LIVE JESUS IN
OUR HEARTS-FOREVER.
GOD BLESS-BOB MC ELROY "53"
BOB MC ELROY

Sunday, November 21, 2010 4:45 PM

Dan and Karen:
Sorry we didn't talk to you at church last nite, but we didn't know
about Dan's diagnosis at that time. Steve happened to get on Facebook and saw Joe's note, Please know that we will be doing lots of
praying for all of you. You've gone thru it before so know what to
expect. It will be tough, but with God's help and everyone's prayers
you will be tougher. I'm so glad you are on this website because we'll
be able to get the updates once we are in AZ. Hang in there.
Howard and Ann Prell

Sunday, November 21, 2010 7:08 PM

Dear Karen and Dan:
You are truly wonderful and courageous friends. Be assured that
you are in my daily thoughts and prayers as you go through your
treatments and day-to-day routines to fight this demon! May you
feel the great love everyone is sending your way.
God Bless you!
With love and prayers! Clara Timmerman

Monday, November 22, 2010 1:48 PM

I too was shocked to hear the news. My thoughts and prayers are with you both. I know you have the strength and believe to carry you through.

> Many blessings,
> Karen Halverson

Monday, November 22, 2010 2:37 PM

Dan:

Want you to know that Jeri and my prayers are with you and Karen. Hope your new doctor will provide some good options for you.

Willard & Jeri Ogren

Monday, November 22, 2010 8:39 PM

Please, God, take charge of Dan's life. Guide him. Hold him in your perfect love and fill all his needs. Please, God, take charge of Karen's life. Guide her. Hold her in your perfect love and fill all her needs.

This is a prayer I start the day with and say as I go through my day—for me and my family and for whoever else needs God's help. I will continue to pray for you to have strength and find some peace in your busy days.

Kathy Hiber

Monday, November 22, 2010 9:48 PM

We will all be thinking and praying for you.

Jerry Bies

Monday, November 22, 2010 10:27 PM

As you know, I've been this road before with Frank and my self. He was my caretaker and he's gone and I'm here. We just never know God's plan. You and all your family are in my prayers and thoughts many times during the day. Your great faith and wonderfully supportive family will be a blessing to you on this journey, my little brother.

I love you. Peg Likar

Monday, November 22, 2010 11:04 PM

Dear Dan and Karen:

As I said in my email to you, I am thinking of you constantly as you through this latest journey. It was a year ago that we were all together in Sioux Falls for Verna's birthday. You did such a wonderful job of getting the family together. My prayers are with you. Thank you for this page so that we can be updated as to your progress.

Love, Ellen Giles

Tuesday, November 23, 2010 12:04 AM

We will be thinking of Dan and you on Wednesday as he has his scans and tests. So glad to hear you have your wonderful kids with you through all of this. They are amazing. You two are people with strong faiths; may this help you to find an inner peace and hope in the days ahead. Good luck with the condo search. It sounds like a good location with a beautiful view.

Have a great Thanksgiving with your family. Hats off to the pie maker!

Sending prayers for good answers and a successful beginning with chemo. Continuing to hold your hand from a distance.

Karen Daniels

Tuesday, November 23, 2010 8:15 AM

Sorry to hear the health report via Mike Heffron. So, here is voice out of the past. I had to check the year book but after 57-years it was not much help! We are hoping that the reports are good and that the treatments are effective. Wife Pat had non-Hodgkins lymphoma in 1995 and radiation did the job so far. We have been retired in Hot Springs Village AR since 1994. We do get back to MN to see some of our kids (3 families), grand kids and 2 GREAT grand kids. The others are in CO, and 2 in TX. This Caring Bridge is a great app. We are getting reports from 2 others at this time.

Again our prayers and best wishes to you, Bill and Pat Gerstner

Tuesday, November 23, 2010 11:19 AM

What a beautiful song that is, Karen, and sung for such a variety of reasons, but never more appropriate than your current trial. I know you and Uncle Dan will courageously meet that challenge...hold your head high, keep hope in your heart, walk on and NEVER alone. We love you and are here to walk for you when you are unable.

Mary (Likar) Starkman

Tuesday, November 23, 2010 4:09 PM

Uncle Dan & Aunt Karen:
We were devastated with the news AND share in your confidence in Christ. HE is the great physician! Our entire church family is praying in agreement for a miracle healing. You are in our thoughts and prayers.

Love You, Roxanne, Dan & Gaby Johnson

Tuesday, November 23, 2010 6:48 PM

So happy you have found such a nice place for the winter. With family close by, you will be surrounded by loving hands. That's good. How nice that people are taking care of your needs on Buskey Bay. I think I may be related to your snow angel. :>)

Take care. Karen Daniels

Tuesday, November 23, 2010 9:52 PM

Glad you have found a good place in Duluth to live temporarily. I won't be visiting you soon as I managed to pick a cold from my roommate last weekend. Want to be sure I'm well as you will be compromised. I will be praying and thinking of you much of the time until I am able to see you. Hope scans etc. went well today. Have a wonderful thanksgiving with your family. I will spend mine with Mary, Scott & family. Love to you all.

Peg Likar

Tuesday, November 23, 2010 11:13 PM

Dan and Karen:
You are in our prayers. May you continue to stay strong, determined, and live your life. I understand you have always been a survivor and that is what we are expecting and praying for regardless of a diagnosis. Many prayers are being extended for you while you beat this.
Greg and Chris Ogren

Wednesday, November 24, 2010 6:13 AM
Dan & Karen:
You will find that there are so many angel's surrounding you. It is so wonderful to know that they are there for you. It seemed like every time I had something to be done, it got done by one of the angel's. Thinking of you and praying everyday for all of you.
Karen Wicklund

Wednesday, November 24, 2010 5:52 PM

Dear Dan and Karen:
What good news you got today! Even in the midst of this difficult time there will certainly be many prayers of thanksgiving, won't there. We're sure glad you have the place in Duluth and don't have to worry about traveling on the winter roads. Remember that many, many people care about you and are praying for you.
With love and prayers, Julie & Jerry Peck

Wednesday, November 24, 2010 6:46 PM

What great news today! We will see you on Saturday, good luck with the first round of Chemo on Friday.
Love you both,
Dan, Ann & Chelle (Collins)

Wednesday, November 24, 2010 8:48 PM

Hoping the best. Bill Gerstner

Wednesday, November 24, 2010 9:11 PM

Great news about the scan & MRI reports! No matter how dark things seem at times, there are always many more things to be thankful for. How appropriate that Thanksgiving Day is tomorrow. I'll be praying for you as you begin the chemotherapy Friday.
Love, Peg Likar

Thursday, November 25, 2010 9:22 AM

Hi Dan, Karen and family. We are glad you are all able to be together. We wish you a Happy Thanksgiving. Our daughters and grandchildren are coming to our home this afternoon and Janet and I are looking forward to being together.
John Ahern

Thursday, November 25, 2010 1:50 PM

Happy Thanksgiving to the Collins clan. My two kids and four grandchildren, Everett and I will be getting together this afternoon to celebrate all the blessings of the past year. Beautiful sunny day here but c-c-c-cold!
Ellen Giles

Thursday, November 25, 2010 3:03 PM

Sending my love to all of you for a very **HAPPY THANKSGIVING!** Good Luck tomorrow Dan; though I am some distance away, you are very close in my heart!
Love & prayers, Mary Peterson

Thursday, November 25, 2010 7:00 PM

Happy Thanksgiving, I wish we could have been there but skype helped us get together which was really cool. Love ya.
Dan Collins

Friday, November 26, 2010 7:15 AM

Dad, I hope all goes well today and we will see you tomorrow.
Love you, Dan

Friday, November 26, 2010 12:20 PM

Happy Thanksgiving to the Collins Family. We're thinking of you during this difficult time. You're in our thoughts & prayers.
Love Dave & Robin Peterson

Friday, November 26, 2010 12:44 PM

Tis black Friday. I did not have to go to the shopping madness. My granddaughter told me of her escapades shopping. She ended up with electric toothbrushes. I can't imagine that she saved that much on toothbrushes. I trust you and the family are enjoying this wonderful time of the year. I wish I could head south. Too much still happening here so I'll tough it out for awhile longer.
Talk at you later. Richard DelMedico

Friday, November 26, 2010 4:15 PM

Praise the Lord! You deserve the special treatment and encouraging news that you've gotten. It's said that as we progress in our life journeys the challenges become greater—but we have a God that never gives us more than we can handle. Your Lord, your family and your friends are here to walk this journey with you. (If you need a lift with the packing and loading, we're only a few minutes away.)
Peace be with you, John and Jeanne Joseph

Friday, November 26, 2010 6:55 PM

Happy Thanksgiving, Dan & Karen (and family) — You are in my thoughts and prayers.
Kim Lakhan

Friday, November 26, 2010 8:24 PM

Mary Lou, Dan and Karen:
I am very bouyed at hearing the wonderful news that the cancer has not spread too pervasively. That is very hopeful. Thank you for your updates, so that we can check in on your news and progress

to date. There really IS something to be said for many prayers and positive thinking. Glad you had a good Thanksgiving. Julie and Gale Mellum

Saturday, November 27, 2010 8:03 AM

Dan and Karen:
We are following your messages everyday. We are so happy that all is going well. You continue in our prayers daily. If there were to be anything you need for us to do, please don't hesitate to ask. Sometimes, people just don't know what to do.
All our love, Tom and Marcia Bouchard

Saturday, November 27, 2010 9:42 AM

"Top of the mornin'" to you, Dan and Karen! I am so glad to hear of the great results after just one day of chemo. That is a blessing indeed. I love the expression, "Praise the Lord" and that is what I'm doing right now.
Julie Mellum

Saturday, November 27, 2010 10:22 AM

Dan ...Well, here it is two days after Mr. Turkey left town and I'm still "all puffed up" ... Hope you and your family had a peaceful and happy day ... Keep plugging and praying ...
Your friend ... Mike Heffron

Saturday, November 27, 2010 1:26 PM

Great picture!! We're glad to hear Dan is more comfortable. The sun is shining here today. Hope it is there, too.
Kathy Hiber

Saturday, November 27, 2010 2:47 PM

Wonderful news!!!!
S Farnady

Saturday, November 27, 2010 3:29 PM

Dear Dan and Karen:
Glad you had such a nice Thanksgiving. A chance for you all to support each other, and have fun together. You have been and will continue to be in our thoughts and prayers. We wish you strength, peace, and understanding, and more positive results from the treatments!
Your friends, Vicki and Dan Knapp

Saturday, November 27, 2010 9:19 PM

Hi Dan & Karen"
So glad things are coming together so nicely for your Northern Winter Trip. Some people go south; you go north and have friends, family, a lake with a view, and the Pickwick right across the street! With an exercise room, pool, & a few more amenities you two definitely know how to make lemonade when handed lemons. In the midst of it all, you strong faiths and love for each other are great models for everyone. Sending prayers for strength to meet each new day ... and ... continuing to hold your hands from a distance.
Karen and Rod Daniels

Sunday, November 28, 2010 6:13 AM

Dan & Karen:
Kitty & I said a prayer for the both of you on Thanksgiving. We're glad to see that Dan is doing better. The condo is a great idea and we hope everything works out. Remember if you need anything please let us know.
Lee Ruska

Thanks so much for posting the information about colds, Dan. I know when my dad was compromised; he received visits from very well intentioned and caring folks who really put him at risk for infection. Another reminder for everyone to get a flu shot if you haven't already done so! Although I wasn't a believer in this for many years, I started getting them so I wouldn't get my dad sick. (I know this was somewhat selfish considering I could have gotten my patients sick, it didn't make the impact until our family was affected.) Hope the move...

Mary Starkman

Monday, November 29, 2010 8:12 AM

It sounds as if things are going well under these trying circumstances. We know the chemo drill very well from the other side of things. You'll get used to the routine of things, so take it just one day at a time. Distractions are a good idea. So glad you had a great Thanksgiving. The Lord does provide, especially at times like these. Ready for another game whenever you are!

Bless you, Ellen Hoeltgen

Tuesday, November 30, 2010 7:14 PM

Dear Dan and Karen:

Karen Wicklund was in the hop today and told us about Dan. We are so sorry to hear this news. Our thoughts and prayers are with you on this journey, there is always hope

Carrie and Nancy-The Beauty Stuga

Wednesday, December 1, 2010 2:47 PM

Dan and Karen:

It was a joy to read about your "vacation" home in Duluth!

Julie and Gale Mellum

Wednesday, December 1, 2010 5:00 PM

Loved your newest photo addition. Take care.

Ellen Giles

Wednesday, December 1, 2010 7:58 PM

Dan & Karen: I hope it is going as well with your health and the challenge of a workout every day, as your apartment fits your needs. Now that is a very poor sentence. My excuse is that it is time to go home for supper. Dan, you are in our thought & prayers. You too, Karen.

Willard & Jeri Ogren

Wednesday, December 1, 2010 9:10 PM

Congratulations on your successful move. How many bedrooms do you have? Sounds wonderful! I'm envious. I love <u>ALL</u> the moods of Lake Superior and watching the ships coming and going. The shipping season will be over sometime after the first of the year so won't be as much traffic. The best part of my 30 day radiation treatments was the view from the windows of the 1st St. Clinic building. I had early morning treatments so got to enjoy fog rising from the lake a lot.

Yes, you do have great kids, as do I. We must have done something right.

Hope Friday's chemo treatment goes as well as the last one.

Love you, Peg Likar

Wednesday, December 1, 2010 10:47 PM

Dear Karen & Dan: Finally I was able to get into your website -I had problems-hence the delay in telling you how sorry I am to hear of your health problems. Your view looking over Lake Superior is certainly as beautiful if not more so than looking over Lake Havasu. You will certainly be in our thoughts and prayers.

Your neighbors on Buskey Bay Dr-Mary & John Lagesse

Wednesday, December 1, 2010 11:12 PM

Aunt Karen and Uncle Dan:

I'm so happy that you were able to find a condo that will more than meet your needs. I love your upbeat positive attitude and your faith. That is what will get you through this. Good luck with the surgery tomorrow.

Caroline Walline

Thursday, December 2, 2010 8:21 AM

Dan and Karen:
What a great website! It is so nice to be able to follow your moves. Yes, you two do have a wonderful family. You certainly did a great job raising them. My cousin and her husband stayed at Beacon Pointe last summer. They, too, raved about it. We're so happy that you have a comfortable place. You both are in our prayers daily. Please don't hesitate to ask for anything. Sometimes, people just don't know what to do. Just let us know. We love you both.
Tom and Marcia Bouchard

Thursday, December 2, 2010 11:30 PM

Happy to hear the move went well. Hope you are settling in comfortably to your new surroundings. It's amazing how a city can quiet down and give people time to feel a calming peace. I think you and Dan find that wherever you happen to be. It's evident in the positiveness you share everyday. Praying that the surgery went well today and tomorrow's chemo will go smoothly. Stay strong and trust.
Karen Daniels

Saturday, December 4, 2010 11:23 AM

Hi Dan, I finally got on your CaringBridge site. Seems they didn't like my password. Glad to see you are getting settled in and it would seem the doctors aren't wasting any time so all you have to do is get well. You are in our prayers just hang in here.
GEORGE & KAY ROSSEZ

Sunday, December 5, 2010 9:45 PM

I'm glad things are still going well and love the picture.
Peg Likar

Monday, December 6, 2010 3:03 PM

Karen and Dan:

What a joy it is to see the photo of you two with the backdrop of Lake Superior. It seems like you are on a delightful vacation, which of course this isn't. Still, you are an inspiration to all of us to see how you are making the best of things. This is truly a gift.

Love, Julie and Gale Mellum

Tuesday, December 7, 2010 3:06 PM

Dan and Karen:
A nice picture! How wonderful for you that your kids are so good to you! You can be so proud of the job you have done. We will follow your postings everyday. God Bless!

Love, Tom and Marcia Bouchard

Tuesday, December 7, 2010 7:27 PM

Hi Dan and Karen:
Just want you to know we are thinking about you and praying for you every day. So glad you had a nice Thanksgiving with your family and that you continue to be surrounded by your great kids and grandchildren. We will be traveling out to Fargo for about five days starting tomorrow. When we return we will contact you and if Dan feels up to it and if we are healthy maybe we can stop up for a visit.

So glad you were able to find such a wonderful place to stay for the winter. One gets addicted to the beautiful view and it must be uplifting for you to wake up every morning to such a lovely vista. I know it is for us. Take care and we'll talk soon.

Sue & John McLennan

Wednesday, December 8, 2010 8:43 AM

Dan and Karen, Just a note to let you know that our thoughts and prayers are constantly with you and will continue to be as we go through this wonderful Christmas season. It sounds as though you are doing as well as you can with the surrounding love of your family and friends which will be a great source of strength.

May God continue to bless you, Ellen Hoeltgen

Friday, December 10, 2010 8:00 AM

Dear Dan and Karen:

Dave and Karen Michaud think of, pray for you, and recall the times we have with you two over the years as the good ones. It sounds Dan, like the coughing might be even tougher than putting the 8-foot window covers on the log home! You will handle both with the internal strength that has helped you make a great life.

We are amazed by the adaptations, and the support group that you have made and created thru your past life. They will serve you well now. We have not done such effective work but do continue to meet the challenges as they progress.

My computer skills have lagged but now seem to have gotten us to your web site, hope they don't break down again. We have put Karen's extensive Santa collection, which has been in the attic for years, on the walls, all flat surfaces, some hangers from above and a tree to follow up, as Molly, John, three grandkids, two dogs, one cat, and miscellaneous smaller creatures are coming for two weeks starting Dec 20. This will be their first winter experience since they moved to Texas six years ago so it should be interesting. Their average temp is in the 80 range so wardrobe and tolerance will both need help.

It's Friday a.m. and Karen wants to be part of St Mike's Christmas fair planning and tomorrow's event so have to go create breakfast and a trip to Iron River. I hope to do better on contact with you in the future than the past. Our love and prayers ride with you.

Dave and Karen Michaud

Friday, December 10, 2010 5:34 PM

Dan and Karen:

We so enjoy reading the journal entries. The pictures are also wonderful. You certainly do have a fantastic support system. The rest of us are using the power of prayer. Our thoughts and love are with you all.

We know you are looking forward to the week end of your get together in the Dells. Robyn and Larry are getting married that Saturday. The Hudacks will be here on that day. It is a small wedding, but the Bishop is performing the ceremony, so it should be extra special.

Please know how much we care and we will continue to be in touch.

Love, Tom and Marcia Bouchard

Friday, December 10, 2010 7:21 PM

Hello Dan and Karen:

We have been following Dan's progress through the CaringBridge site and are happy that Dan's first round of chemo treatment went well. We are praying for you both and are glad you are in the Duluth condo vs. commuting back and forth from Iron River for Dan's treatment. Your planned family trip to Wisconsin Dells sounds like a great January get-together. We hope the highways are in good shape for your travel.

We are currently visiting our daughter and family in Houston, Texas and will head to Tucson, AZ next week. After watching the weather channel's coverage of the Duluth and Twin Cities areas today, we won't joke about your weather.

Warm Regards, John and Pat Hancock

Friday, December 10, 2010 8:09 PM

Dan and Karen:

Good to hear there is hope that the vocal cord adjustment may help your voice, Dan. Since everyone always wonders if lung cancer patients were smokers, it was good to read that history too. But please know, as many people are just starting to realize, that wood smoke is even more of a factor in lung cancer these days. It pervades everyone's life to varying degrees because it is so common from outdoor wood furnaces, recreational burning, indoor fireplaces and smoke from restaurant wood grills. This is causing a huge upswing in lung cancers even in people who have never smoked. Please know also that if you can avoid breathing wood smoke when you are outdoors, you will enhance your chances for recovery and better quality of life. It is so heartwarming to read about your progress.

Love, Julie and Gale Mellum

Saturday, December 11, 2010 7:43 AM

Good Morning Dan and Karen:
Thank you for the updates on Dan. Jerry and I want you to know that you are in our prayers. Enjoy each day you have. Our wishes to you and your family for a Merry Christmas and Blessed Holiday season.
God Bless - Jerry & Judy Darwin

Saturday, December 11, 2010 9:17 AM

Dan and Karen:
What a joy it was to see that wonderful photo that captured it all of Mary Lou walking down the aisle with her beloved daddy. Dan is the man!
Julie Mellum

Saturday, December 11, 2010 10:04 AM

Wow! If you like snow, this is the place to be today. We caught a load overnight and it keeps coming. Prediction was 8-12 inches and for once, I think the weather-jerk may be right. Have not heard (yet) how it is north of here. You may be catching it as well.
The old timers had lunch yesterday at DeGideo's down on 7th. About 60 or so from Cretin, the Academy, DeLaSalle, Monroe, etc. John Ryan brought a bunch of photos from Cretin days. Caught your "mug" on a couple.
Several asked for you and send their best. They're computer illiterate so don't catch CaringBridge which is a great site for family and friends. I was especially pleased to see Mike Scott who is looking great (and talkative as ever). He had a long and difficult siege of lung and prostate cancer, but appears on the mend.
Keep plugging Dan. We're all pulling for you and expect you back for the Cretin monthly lunch soon.
Mike Heffron

Saturday, December 11, 2010 10:30 AM

What a darling family picture.
Kathy Hiber

Sunday, December 12, 2010 9:47 AM

Well Dan, your bag is never empty! I am staggered by your needlepoint and versatility in all things. And by your wonderful and abiding faith. Karen, it is such a joy to read all your postings and updates. Thanks for your address. I see you have had almost one THOUSAND visits to your site.
Hatari! Julie Mellum

Monday, December 13, 2010 9:48 AM

Hi Dan and Karen, I so enjoyed talking to you on Thursday and getting an update on how things are going. I hope the book gives you as much comfort as it did my sister, I'll bet you have a spectacular view of the lake with all this frigid weather, Try and stay warm and know you're in our prayers. with our best wishes.
Carol and Cal Foster

Tuesday, December 14, 2010 8:22 AM

Dan and Karen, I, too, have been giving Tom haircuts since 1967. We can certainly understand that this last haircut had to be very difficult. But, we know as you do, that no matter what kind of haircut Dan has, he is a handsome man and you two are a beautiful couple. That is why your children are all so good looking.
You continue in our prayers daily. Your strength and faith carries you.
All our love, Tom and Marcia Bouchard

Tuesday, December 14, 2010 8:38 AM

Karen and Dan, The haircutting story is wonderfully poignant. It brings back some funny memories for us, too. I'm cutting Tom's hair (singular) now. As we all know, Tom has very few hairs, so it makes the job easy. We continue to follow your postings and are heartened that things are going well. Bless you both. You remain in our hearts and prayers.
Tom and Ellen Hoeltgen

Tuesday, December 14, 2010 9:20 AM

Karen, everything you write is interesting and thoughtful. I got a kick out of your saying you gave Dan a "buzz." It was neat to read that your talents include great "tonsorial" skills—who would have known, had it not been for this. Your bag is never empty. If you'd like to cut my mop, I'd love to hire you at the lake!
    Julie Mellum

Tuesday, December 14, 2010 6:29 PM

Hi Dan and Karen: Well, I'll make 1 more entry before we leave snowy, cold (-10 this morning) Iron River for the winter. As I was reading Karen's updates and thinking about years past I remembered our wonderful trip to Vienna with the Northwestern Community Choir and the video you made and then made a copy for me. You and Jack Flynn were two who had a great friendship in and out of the choir. Also think back of when our boys were in school and Little League baseball together. Those were the days — right? Anyway, we want to wish you a successful chemo treatment session. We'll keep praying for that to happen. Have a wonderful time on your family trip in Jan. and also over the Christmas season. Prayers will continue on the Hot Line To Heaven from AZ and I'll be putting your name in our Book of Intentions at our church down there.
    God Bless Howard and Ann Prell

Wednesday, December 15, 2010 7:02 AM

Hello Dan & Karen:
So glad to hear the chemo treatments are going well. The meds they have now really help to manage the side effects! Dan—I like your new haircut. I used to have one just like it. I think that hair is really overrated anyway!!! It's nice to just put on a hat and go. Actually, before you know it, it will grow back & you will barely remember not having any! Your new home looks beautiful from the pics. What views! Nice to experience the big lake for a while. Take care and as always, you are in our prayers.
    Chris Ogren

Wednesday, December 15, 2010 8:53 AM

Dan the Man looks pretty good with the new buzz and all. Your grandson Nate is a handsome dude, too. One must ask how tall is he? And what a marvelous build! (I'm old enough I can get by saying that)!

Julie Mellum

Wednesday, December 15, 2010 9:26 AM

Dan & Karen: It's great to follow everything in your journal. We have you <u>all</u> in our thoughts and prayers. Merry Christmas & Happy New Year to all your family!!!

Steve, Denise, Michael & Claire Peterson

Wednesday, December 15, 2010 2:09 PM

Dan:

As we have been in Mexico the past week and Jeri had me in 2 catholic churches and it was all in Spanish so no need to pay attention therefore a few Lutheran prayers in English were said for you and Karen from the pew with a background music from an electric guitar during communion. Very easy to says prayers in that environment.

Willard Ogren

Wednesday, December 15, 2010 2:40 PM

There's something sexy about a bald headed man. I should know I had one and when the hair grew in again, it wasn't quite as gray. Heard a joke once that a man who is bald on the top of his head is a thinker; one who is bald on the back of his head is a lover and one who is completely bald thinks he's a lover.

Peg Likar

Wednesday, December 15, 2010 7:00 PM

You do look like you did when you were in the army. Just the hair color is different. Glad to hear things are going well.

Ellen Giles

Thursday, December 16, 2010 5:20 PM

Hi Dan & Karen:
Everything sounds like it's going good for the both of you. Keep up your fight Dan! I talked to Karen Nystrom, Mike's mom (Jennifer's husband) who was a nurse. She told me of her husband's work companion who had stage 4 lung cancer and fought it with chemo and won...She is now 84 and doing wonderfully.... We hope that the doctor's can find the problem with your vocal cords and you can get talking again.
With love Brian & Sharon Farnady

Friday, December 17, 2010 12:53 PM

Dan, you will be in my prayers every day. You beat this once and, with treatment and prayers, you will beat this again. Now, about the chemo, I can fully attest after almost 50 years of sparseness on the top, that bald is beautiful! You have a great spouse and family and also have many friends who are all with you on your journey to beat this thing. God is with you. Joe Di Cola

Friday, December 17, 2010 6:36 PM

Dan and Karen:
Our hearts and prayers are with you and your family as you wage your battle with cancer. With the support of your family and friends, your warriors are all lined up beside you. What a wonderful idea to move closer to the clinic and skip the snowy drive. We will follow your progress and continue to send healing thoughts your way.
Your summertime Buskey Bay neighbors,
Glenn and Susie (Cheever) Viggiano

Saturday, December 18, 2010 5:30 PM

Hi Dan and Karen:
It is nice to "meet" your grandson, Nate. He sounds like a wonderful young man. We are in Neenah getting ready for Christmas with our son Tim, wife Sherry and our five grandchildren.
The weather is milder here, so it has been nice to get our shopping

and errands done. Last night we went out for fish with some old friends, it was a nice evening. We are glad the chemo is going well. It looks like your place on Lake Superior is beautiful.

Love, John and Jeanne Joseph

Sunday, December 19, 2010 10:03 AM

Hello Dan and Karen:

I hope this note continues to find you doing well. You have been in my thoughts and prayers and I will continue to send positive thoughts your way. It's Karen Lee (Bies, Myers) or whatever. I apologize, but somehow I missed knowing about your website. I have printed it out and will show it to mom and dad and forward it to my family members. It's times like this it would be nice for mom and dad to have a computer. We've at least moved them into cell phones. We all wish you the very best during this amazing journey of love, faith and patience.

Lots of love, hugs and smiles,

Your niece, Karen Lee

Sunday, December 19, 2010 11:41 AM

Glad to hear you are having a good week, Dan. Karen, the Nativity scene is lovely. Merry Christmas.

Kathy Hiber

Sunday, December 19, 2010 4:01 PM

Dan and Karen:

It was so good to talk with you the other evening. I am happy to know that the treatments are going well, and that you have found a place closer to the medical facilities.

My prayers are with you every day, and I pray for all the best for you in 2011.

Love to both of you,

Joe Di Cola

Monday, December 20, 2010 9:11 AM

Dear Dan and Karen:

Every time I read one of your journal entries I come away with a peaceful, warm feeling. In the midst of chemo, both of you are inspiring to so many through your love, care, and appreciation for family and each other. These gifts you share now are true gifts of this season. In return, we hope you are feeling the prayers and support from all who write in your guestbook each day. Growing up with this mom, the organ lady, my kids always used to say Christmas time was one of my "State Tourneys" ... lots of practicing and services (games). I agreed, but always told them, I never had to wonder who the winner would be. That's Christmas ... the season of hope, wonder, and a promise that no matter what, "All Will Be Well". As I play today and in the days ahead, that will be my prayer for both of you. Hope you can feel it!

Love, Karen (Cheever) Daniels

Monday, December 20, 2010 1:55 PM

Hi Dan and Karen:

That picture of Nate looks just like his Dad. How great that you are able to see all those kids. That helps! You continue to look good, Dan. Keep up your great attitude. If you have any time when you get to the Dells, give Mary Lou a call. She and Larry are not coming for the wedding, but their kids are, so they will probably be alone at that time. Tom talked to her the other day and she isn't doing the best right now. She has quite a bit of pain and is taking some morphine pills.

We hope you all have a wonderful Christmas. Our love to your entire family.

Thomas & Marsha Bouchard

Monday, December 20, 2010 2:26 PM

Can't wait to see you this weekend! We love you!
Colleen Collins

Wednesday, December 22, 2010 11:13 AM

Dear Uncle Dan and Aunt Karen:

I am grateful my sister Karen informed me of your website. I have read your journal and am thankful that you have a ton of help and support. What a beautiful setting for you to live in while you are needing to stay close to doctors. I can only image how peaceful it is while Uncle Dan is resting at home. You raised your children well, they are honoring their Mother and Father in the best way possible. (Grandkids too!) I want you to know that I will continue to pray for all of you. (As are my Mom and Dad. Mom was very upset receiving the news that her baby brother was facing cancer again.) Your faith a wonderful example to all of us.

Love, Beth (Bies) Huonder

Wednesday, December 22, 2010 6:07 PM

Merry Christmas to you, Dan and Karen, and to your wonderful family! We have been blessed with your friendship for these many years, and we know that God will bless you this holiday season.

Peace be with you, Tom and Ellen Hoeltgen

Thursday, December 23, 2010 1:38 PM

Dear Dan & Karen:

Just a note to wish you both a Merry Christmas! We realize that these might not be the best of circumstances but hope you enjoy the holiday with your family.

Jim and Charlotte Selgeby

Thursday, December 23, 2010 6:30 PM

Dan: Hope the email I sent has been getting through as Karen knows how limited my computer skills are. The prayers said in church in Mexico must have been heard as I see when I got home you had some good days. Hope you and Karen have a Merry Christmas with family and friends. Will continue the prayers in the USA also.

Willard & Jeri Ogren

Thursday, December 23, 2010 10:38 PM

Dear Dan and Karen:

You continue to be an inspiration to those who know and care about you. In spite of this difficult road that you are traveling, we know that you have found many, many things for which to be thankful. We are praying that this Christmas will be special for you and your family in many ways!

Jerry and Julie Peck

Friday, December 24, 2010 9:08 AM

Merry Christmas to the whole Collins family. I'm so impressed at your closeness and devotion to one another. You are an inspiration to us! May your blessings abound.

Julie and Gale Mellum

Friday, December 24, 2010 1:12 PM

Dan & Karen:

FYI I received the Thank You from John Hancock yesterday. I will read it at next months meeting. Kitty talked to Punch today & we thought maybe a Sat. after the first of the year the three of us could come up to visit the two of you. I didn't know if we should put this message on this site or your e-mail but decided to use this site. We're glad to hear that everything is going as well as it can at this time. You're both in our prayers every day & we would like to come up and see you. Kitty & I want to wish you & your family a very Merry Christmas & a Happy New Year.

Lee Ruska

Tuesday, December 28, 2010 9:01 AM

Hi, Dan:

Very happy to know that the anti-nausea meds are working well. Also glad to hear that this is being treated aggressively by your going to chemo more often. I think the best news is today's posting that says how much better you are feeling in terms of pain, breathing, etc. Sounds like Christmas was blessed by family and friends.

Do say hello to John and Sue when you see them. We belonged to the same parish in Fargo. If I remember correctly, they also have a view of Lake Superior. Also, hi to Gale and Julie and to Mary Peterson. Believe it or not, we are to be in the low 30s for a nighttime temp by Thursday! It will feel like Duluth! Know that you are daily in my thoughts and prayers and, being the fighter you are, you will conquer this. And, I do have to close with some comment on the Vikings (your hat notwithstanding)—RETIRE Brett Favre!

Love to all,

Joe Di Cola

Tuesday, December 28, 2010 12:49 PM

Glad to hear that the treatments are working. Continued good progress for the NEW YEAR.

Bill Gerstner

Tuesday, December 28, 2010 8:47 PM

Dan, sorry to hear about your illness. Seems like so much of it is going around these days. I was at our 50th class reunion but none since. As one gets older it gets a little harder to get around. Our prayers and thoughts are with you and your family.

Joe and Kathy Filipczak Evansville, IN

Tuesday, December 28, 2010 11:02 PM

Dan: Glad to learn that things are getting more comfortable for you. Keep up the good fight and know our prayers are with you.

Jay Brooks

Saturday, January 1, 2011 9:37 AM

Happy - HAPPY - New Year! May each day be better than the day before. We are so very glad to hear how well Dan is doing. We thank God for the blessings he gives us each day! And those gifts serve to remind us that we need to ask - through prayer.

Al and Karen Nicol

Monday, January 3, 2011 10:49 AM

Hi, Dan, I hope this 3rd of January finds you doing good like the posting said on Dec. 28. It is hard to believe that it is 2011. Now I only have to remember to date checks correctly. My prayers continue to be with you as you proceed with your course of treatment, and that your health will improve. One thing that will help is the strength you have shown through all of this. You are truly blessed in Karen and in your children who bring their own strengths and faith into your fight. There is no question that, with them by your side, the battle can be won.

It has been in the upper 20s the last few nights, but I am hoping that the temps will moderate some. Living in the desert I think thins your blood and while daytime 40s in Illinois would call for shorts and t-shirts, it is not the case here.

I look forward to hearing about your progress and will stay in touch.

Love to all, Joe Di Cola

Tuesday, January 4, 2011 9:03 AM

Continuing to pray for you while down here in AZ. Certainly pray that the anti nausea med helps and for a safe a fun trip for you this weekend.

Howard and Ann Prell

Tuesday, January 4, 2011 9:35 AM

Dan, it took me a while to find you on CaringBridge. Wasn't putting in your middle initial? Judy Darwin sent me the link so will be reading your story from now on. I thought your family picture by the lake was just great! What a wonderful family—I am sure their support is a blessing to you and Karen now.

My prayers have been with you every day and I am sure you can feel all the prayers of so many friends and family. As you go thru the chemo treatments I hope our prayers will help. We will be leaving soon but will have my laptop and access to this site. I will check it often and hope by the time we return the most difficult days will be behind you and you will be well on the road to recovery.

Love, Bill and Bev Lindsey

Tuesday, January 4, 2011 10:09 AM

Praying this week will bring good results with the meds. Think of all the fun you will have at the Dells on the weekend. May those warm thoughts carry you through to that great family of yours. I don't know them, but can tell they are an amazing family, full of support for you. Just forget about those Vikings! Set your sights on the Twins! Sending prayers and good thoughts your way.

Karen Daniels

Tuesday, January 4, 2011 10:10 AM

Hi, Dan:

Hope the new dosage of anti-nausea continues to work and that you first week back at chemo treatments goes well for you.

Have a great time with your family at The Dells. How wonderful to have so many family members at this reunion! What a blessing!

You are in my prayers and thoughts.

Joe Di Cola

Tuesday, January 4, 2011 2:30 PM

I forgot that you were having the chemo a day early this week. Hope all goes well so that you can fully enjoy your time with all the children & grandchildren in the Dells.

Peg Likar

Tuesday, January 4, 2011 7:57 PM

It was good to see and talk to you both on Skype tonight. It looks like the new anti-nausea medication is working. See you Friday night in the Dells.

Dan Collins

Wednesday, January 5, 2011 10:03 AM

Just want you both to know that we were successful in signing in and got the latest news via Carebridge. Thank you for this great link to you so that you know that we are thinking of you and praying for all involved with your care.

Clyde and Mariam Snider

Wednesday, January 5, 2011 9:07 PM

Dan and Karen, it was so heartwarming to see the bear in your photo by the window! Gosh, I just hate to hear of your nausea and being unable to eat much, Dan. Our prayers are with you both as we hope things will ease up for you. Have a wonderful time with your family in the Dells and may you feel well enough to enjoy it, Dan.
Love, Julie and Gale Mellum

Wednesday, January 5, 2011 10:14 PM

Dan, It was great seeing You and Karen last Thurs. Keep up the good fight. We'll enjoy a pontoon ride this summer. Gale Mellum

Thursday, January 6, 2011 12:18 AM

Ours thoughts & prayers continue to be with you... We hope that you will feel just great when it is time to visit with your family in the Dells...
Happy New Year
Brian & Sharon Farnady

Thursday, January 6, 2011 12:12 PM

Aunt Karen and Uncle Dan:
Hope things are better. I would be happy to make soup and add additional calories if you think this is something you might eat as well as put on pounds. We use a lot of aroma therapy for nausea in our department. Try sniffing some peppermint or ginger when the nausea first starts. Can't hurt, might help! I truly hope you enjoy your adventure with the Collins clan. Safe travels. Perhaps I can get Mom over to see you in the next couple weeks. We'll see how you are feeling.
Love, Mary Starkman

Thursday, January 6, 2011 10:54 PM

Hi Dan and Karen, sorry that your meds are not more friendly, but guess that if they work they are worth some agony. We have a hard time picturing the Dells this time of year, but will remember

Apostle Islands formations and hope that's it. We enjoyed almost two weeks with our Texas family (molly, john, sydney, dexter, logan, and many pets, and their joy over first real snow was a real treat. Hope that your weekend goes well, no weather road thrills and that you feel good enough to enjoy the time.

Happy New Year from Dave and Karen Michaud

Friday, January 7, 2011 8:46 AM

Have a safe trip and wonderful "holiday" with all your family. I hope Dan continues to eat well and enjoy his favorite foods. Howard asks about him and I pass on what I read here and on Facebook.

Love, Karen Nicol

Sunday, January 9, 2011 11:03 AM

Hope this Sunday morn. that you are on your way to recovery. Our prayers and thoughts are with you. May you respond well with treatment and enjoy life again.

Clyde&Mariam Snider

Monday, January 10, 2011 2:09 PM

As I am sure you know—You both have been in our prayers and on our church prayer list.

Love, Bob and Kay Peterson

Monday, January 10, 2011 5:29 PM

Dan and Karen:
It was so good seeing you both. You both look really good. We sure enjoyed our visit. Mary Lou called this morning and said they had a great visit. We're so happy that your weekend was so wonderful. You have an amazing family. We'll be in touch. Keep up your fantastic attitude.

Love, Tom and Marcia Bouchard

Monday, January 10, 2011 5:30 PM

Dan and Karen, so glad you had such a great time in the Dells.

We pass it on the highway often, but haven't been there in years. It's great to hear that you're doing so well. We continue to pray for you and your family. Bless you both,

Tom and Ellen Hoeltgen

Monday, January 10, 2011 7:54 PM

Glad you had such great family time!!! Also happy that the chemo isn't causing such severe side effects. Prayers continue.

Ann Prell

Monday, January 10, 2011 8:44 PM

Hello Dan and Karen:

Glad to hear that your trip to Wisconsin Dells was a good one with your family. It would have been great to see Dan do the water slide. Pat and I continue to offer our prayers for you both even though we are separated by many miles.

The terrible event here in Tucson last Saturday morning has left everyone in this area quite shaken. Two of the persons involved attend the church we attend. One was the Federal Judge John Roll, who was killed. He attended Saturday morning Mass at 8 AM and then went to meet the Congresswoman at her citizen forum. The other man was a retired Colonel who helped subdue the gunman. It proves that you never know what is going to happen next as we go through our lives.

Take Care, John and Pat Hancock

Tuesday, January 11, 2011 10:24 AM

Hi Dan and Karen:

Sounds like you had a wonderful time in the Dells. Also sounds like the treatment is going well. Good news!

John Ahern

Tuesday, January 11, 2011 12:12 PM

Such a wonderful holiday with the family! It makes **me** happy. Thank you for sharing! May the good days continue.

Karen Nicol

Tuesday, January 11, 2011 12:57 PM

It sounds like you had a wonderful trip. I'm so glad Dan felt well and that the chemo went well last week.

Peg Likar

Tuesday, January 11, 2011 6:19 PM

Dear Dan:

We will keep you in our prayers at this difficult time. Karen was such a supportive friend when I needed her this past year. Keep up the good attitude it is half of the battle. We only met that one time at the reunion but I knew that you Karen had made a wonderful choice in you as a husband.

Carol (gillic) Dellise Carol and Buddy Dellise

Wednesday, January 19, 2011 6:16 PM

What wonderful news! We're thrilled for you. Keep up the good work. You remain in our thoughts and prayers!!!!

Tom and Ellen Hoeltgen

Wednesday, January 19, 2011 6:39 PM

What great news, Dan. We will continue to pray and you continue to fight. We'll see you at the Lake in May.

Gale Mellum

Wednesday, January 19, 2011 6:41 PM

Amazing, but believable! We do have a God who watches over us, and ... prayers do work. You must be thrilled, so grateful, and very relieved. Doctors will keep close watch and do what's necessary. Now you do something special to celebrate! How about a Sammy's Pizza!!!!! Think of me when you're eating it. :>) Continuing to hold you in prayer.

Sending hugs from a distance.

Karen Daniels

Wednesday, January 19, 2011 7:27 PM

God Bless Dan and the whole family. You have been in my thoughts and prayers since I found out about Dan's illness. I am so sorry to hear the struggles you have had to endure. I have been keeping up with the journal updates and have been praying.

It is sooo great to hear that Dan is doing well!!! This is a very hard struggle for Dan and the family. Dr Lalich is an EXCELLENT Doctor! (He was the same one Mom had)

Please take care! Dan, Karen and all the rest of the family!! You are in and will be in my thoughts and prayers!! Stay Strong and God Bless!!!

Praying for you and your family.

Sheila and JT Wilcox

Wednesday, January 19, 2011 7:36 PM

What terrific news!!! Will continue to pray for all of you.

Howard and Ann Prell

Wednesday, January 19, 2011 7:43 PM

Dear Karen and Dan:

It is oh, so wonderful to hear your good news! Yes, a miracle! Why is it that we sometimes need reminders that they do indeed happen. I loved hearing that Dan went down the big slide at the Dells. What a joy that must have been for all of you!

You continue to be in our thoughts and prayers. We certainly won't forget prayers of thanksgiving for Dan's present state of health!

Sending hugs from AZ, Julie and Jerry Peck

Wednesday, January 19, 2011 8:17 PM

Dear Dan and Karen:

What wonderful news. A miracle has happened and we are so grateful. May God continue to bless you. We are speechless.

Love, John and Jeanne Joseph

Wednesday, January 19, 2011 9:21 PM

DAN, GREAT REPORT AND INFORMATION. YOU ARE ONE TOUGH SON-OF-A-GUN. KEEP UP THE GREAT RECOVERY AND YOUR SPIRIT. WE ARE WITH YOU. BOB MC ELROY "53"
BOB MC ELROY

Wednesday, January 19, 2011 9:33 PM

What a great day! I am so glad I was a part of it. The coincidence of my appointment with Dr. Lalich just prior to Dan's was the first miracle. In reflection it was not a "co"incidence, but a "God" incidence. When you finished the appointment and Dan came out to the waiting room to tell me the news of no tumor or nodes present on the CT scan, I didn't believe him at first. This is truly a miracle and I praise God for it but will continue to hold him (and all of you) in prayer that the present situation continues. Karen, it was so good that we'd planned lunch together. I enjoyed it very much. We'll do it again with Dan when he regains his appetite.
Peg Likar

Wednesday, January 19, 2011 9:53 PM

Dear Dan and Karen:
What wonderful news. The power of faith in God speaks for it self. Continue the joyful walk.
Carol and Lloyd Dellise

Wednesday, January 19, 2011 10:23 PM

To the Collins Family ~ My heart soars for all of you as you digest this amazing news! It has been my privilege to follow your journey through this site. I believe that not only have all the prayers been heard, but this miracle has also been fueled by family love and support! Rejoicing w/you,
A SSP/CG friend of Pat's...classmate of Dan's.
Lori Campbell

Thursday, January 20, 2011 8:05 AM

May your healing continue and the Lord will always be with you.
Mariam Snider

Thursday, January 20, 2011 9:15 AM

Dan and Karen:
I was overjoyed to read about the cancer being gone in the
lungs—that truly is amazing! You have been very brave, Dan, and
you too, Karen. Your deep faith has surely sustained you and helped
you. For sure our prayers will continue. Keep up that dogged determination, Dan! And think of Atlas and my deliberate, if lame, pun.
Julie Mellum

Thursday, January 20, 2011 9:27 AM

This is the best news ever! We will continue to pray for you and
your family....
Love.
The Farnady's

Thursday, January 20, 2011 11:01 AM

Wonderful News! A very encouraging medical report.
John and Janet Ahern

Thursday, January 20, 2011 3:20 PM

What great news. I'm all smiles. I think I'll go down to the local
pub and have a stiff drink on that. HERE'S TO YA !!
Salute! Dick DelMedico

Thursday, January 20, 2011 7:03 PM

Miracle of miracles!! We are so , so happy. God bless you all!!
Thomas Bouchard

Thursday, January 20, 2011 7:10 PM

Hi, Dan:

I've thought of you often in recent months, but haven't been able to get on CaringBridge until now when I've heard from several CHS classmates. Obviously, the word of your remission is breathtaking. Know that your in our prayers and we share your and your family's joy at this recent news.

Charles Eldredge

Friday, January 21, 2011 9:00 AM

Dear Karen and Dan:

We just read the most recent posting regarding Dan's doctor's report and we are very happy for you both. It is evident that the power of prayer has intervened for Dan. We will continue to keep you both in our prayers through this crucial period of treatment.

Warm Regards, John and Pat Hancock

Friday, January 21, 2011 7:45 PM

What wonderful news! Bill and I are traveling and will most definitely continue our prayers. We appreciate knowing of Dan's progress and will watch for your updates on CaringBridge.

Bev Lindsey

Saturday, January 22, 2011 1:34 PM

How wonderful! I cannot tell you how happy this makes me! Your photo of the two-part rainbow looks to me like a rare phenomena (I'll have to look up the name and get back to you.) It's related to northern lights and is only very rarely seen and not explained. Years ago a friend saw it and related it to a message from God. I'll get back to you.

Karen Nicol

Tuesday, January 25, 2011 11:10 AM

Our thoughts and prayers are for your healing soon.
Clyde & Mariam Snider

Tuesday, January 25, 2011 12:21 PM

Dan and Karen:

This has been quite a saga for all of you, but Dan, you're such a tough guy. You're all strong, that's for sure. That voice box sounds like a real help, but I have a feeling that the less you talk the sooner you may recover? Our prayers are with you, for if anyone deserves to make a smashing recovery it is you, Dan. It is marvelous that the cancer is gone there. Keep up your good work.

Julie and Gale Mellum

Tuesday, January 25, 2011 1:12 PM

Dan & Karen:

So happy for you both! The combination of determination and prayers has worked again! I know something about what you have been thru and the feelings you have as you turned the corner but I certainly didn't have any where near the experience you two have had. Keep up the good work, having cancer as a memory is a good feeling!

LeRoy Hanson

Tuesday, January 25, 2011 1:30 PM

I am glad to here that there is a new plan for the nausea! EAT PAPA EAT!

Love ya, Dan

Wednesday, January 26, 2011 10:21 AM

Dan…. "You don't choose your family. They are God's gift to you, as you are to them."— Desmond Tutu

Thinking of you with all my love,

Tambrey Collins

Sunday, January 30, 2011 6:54 PM

Sending prayers for relief from the chemo. It can't be any fun. So sorry you have to endure this, Dan. Know your strong faith and "Faithful" wife, Karen, will see you through yet another hurdle.

Think with the end in sight.

Wishing God's peace and comfort, Karen Daniels

Sunday, January 30, 2011 7:13 PM

Hope things go better for you this week.
Clyde&Mariam Snider

Sunday, January 30, 2011 11:21 PM

Dan and family — Thanks for the update. It's tough to hear that you're feeling so bad. Know you're in our prayers.
Charles Eldredge

Tuesday, February 1, 2011 9:12 AM

Dear Dan & Karen:
Sure hope this change in medication helps. I've been dehydrated before and that alone is enough to make you feel awful! We'll be praying that you've turned the corner and are on your way to feeling much better. Those chemo drugs have to be so powerful to do what they do and as you well know, it is such a balancing act to find the right combination. We're thinking of both of you and praying for a "fabulous February."
Sending love & prayers, Julie & Jerry Peck

Tuesday, February 1, 2011 9:47 AM

Yeaaaa. Glad the treatment worked. Praying for more successes.
Ann Prell

Tuesday, February 1, 2011 10:34 AM

Glad to hear Dan is more comfortable.
Kathy Hiber

Tuesday, February 1, 2011 11:13 AM

Good Morning:
So nice to hear about the new cook for breakfast. Hope the days

continue to keep improving.

    Carol and Buddy Dellise

Wednesday, February 2, 2011 10:19 AM

Dan and Karen:

We are in St George, UT now and so glad we can keep up-to-date on your progress thru the Carinbridge Website. Enjoyed looking at your pictures again—saw that Dan went down the water slide at the Dells! I have done that several times with Taylor and Allie and therefore appreciate your adventurous spirit! We go to a marvelous church here in St George and will keep the prayers coming - it sounds like they are helping.

    Bev Lindsey

Wednesday, February 2, 2011 12:27 PM

I'd say the good news about Dan's nausea subsiding and Karen's weight loss are wonderful. However, Karen, that's one heck of a way to do it. Enjoyed our visit yesterday a lot and so glad to see Dan looking like he's feeling good. Sorry Carly was scared of your speech enhancement equipment. Prayers continue for you both.

    Peg Likar

Friday, February 4, 2011 9:45 PM

When there is a report (ie, Feb 1) that says you feel better, your followers feel much better. Keep up the attitude and the good work. Karen is now in TX at Molly's home and being treated like visiting royalty. I'll be joining her about Feb 23 and then will go on to Palm Resaca. I've been trying to catch up with the duties that just didn't have time before she flew out and new ones keep cropping before old stuff is finished so I may be losing ground. My self imposed break is over so I had better get back to work. Keep up your good work.

    Dave Michaud

Sunday, February 6, 2011 4:33 PM

Dan and Karen:
We are following your progress always. You are in our prayers. Just know we are thinking of all of you. Will email soon. God Bless.
Love, Thomas & Marcia Bouchard

Sunday, February 6, 2011 7:47 PM

Dan and Karen:
I just saw your slide show again—what a treat. I love the old photos as well as the new. Glad to hear about the hope for less nausea after the next chemo treatments—I pray that this will be so and that good results will be gotten. Rest up, Dan! You surely need it and may quiet and peace be yours for this next "leg."
Cheers from Julie and Gale Mellum

Monday, February 7, 2011 8:48 AM

What a journey you two are on these days. Your positive attitudes are so inspirational for all of us. You truly believe and trust in this familiar saying, "If God leads you to it, He will bring you through it." Prayers for just that in the days ahead, hoping you will glide through them with peace and calm. Thanks for the updates. We hope you feel all the strength and encouragement coming from all who travel with you.
Karen and Rod Daniels

Wednesday, February 9, 2011 7:21 PM

I am glad to hear that you are taking a break, quality of time has to come into play. See you soon!
Love you both, Dan & Ann Collins

Wednesday, February 9, 2011 10:22 PM

Oh Dan & Karen, I'm feeling so sad that you have felt so bad. Sounds like the latest plan makes sense. Hope the fluids and medication today helped. Your are never out of my prayers and thoughts. I know God will carry you through. I love you both.
Peg Likar

Thursday, February 10, 2011 6:03 AM

Dear Dan & Karen:

Think of you and praying for you every day. The power of pray is so great. Without all the prayers that I received I know I would not be here today. Hope the remission last forever. I will be at St. Luke's on the 15th Feb. for follow-up surgery. Will be there for 5-7 days. If you are around there at that time be sure to stop in to see me.

Karen Wicklund

Thursday, February 10, 2011 8:10 AM

We are praying that you health will continue to improve.
Clyde & Mariam Snider

Thursday, February 10, 2011 8:27 AM

Hi Dan and Karen:

Just read your latest update and pray that this break from chemo will help Dan get his strength back and aid him in starting to feel better. We pray for you both everyday and when he starts feeling well again we look forward to another visit with you. Again, if there is anything we can do, please call on us.

Sue and John McLennan

Thursday, February 10, 2011 10:04 AM

Hi, Dan:

I was glad to see that the chemo is being put off until you start getting your strength back. Once that happens and you feel better again, with less nausea and balance issues, you can eat better and get the nourishment you need. The continued prayers that are said on your behalf and God's blessings from above will keep you in remission and, ideally, there will be no need for chemo in the immediate future. God bless you, Dan, for being you and for your courage and determination, and for being the fighter you are.

Joe Di Cola

Thursday, February 10, 2011 12:27 PM

Still with you, Dan, and with your family, in thoughts and prayers. Sounds like your vacation from treatment is the way to go—for now and, hopefully, for good.
Charlie Eldredge, Cretin '53

Friday, February 11, 2011 8:43 AM

Our thoughts and prayers are still with you Dan & Karen, hoping for a speedy recovery and feeling a lot better soon.
With Love Brian & Sharon F. Farnady

Friday, February 18, 2011 6:27 PM

Thank you for all your up-dates. This is wonderful news and proof that prayers really do work! We will keep on praying.
Bev Lindsey

Friday, February 18, 2011 8:11 PM

Great to hear that dad is doing better! Love to both of you!
Colleen Collins

Saturday, February 19, 2011 7:57 AM

Dan and Karen:
So glad that you're off treatment and the nausea is resolving. Keep fighting...you have a wonderful family and a lot of friends in your corner. So sorry that we've been slow on the uptake lately. We've had some recent problems with our daughter, but she's now on treatment and doing better. We all seem to have our crosses to bear, and you're bearing yours with such dignity and love. Keep it up.
Tom and Ellen Hoeltgen

Saturday, February 19, 2011 9:05 AM

Good Morning Karen and Dan:
So happy to hear things are going well.
Keep warm, Carol Dellise

Wednesday, February 23, 2011 8:24 AM

That's wonderful news! It's good that you've been able to venture out and take some nice drives to Iron River. We will look forward to seeing you in July! We pray for speedy recovery Dan.
Brian & Sharon Farnady

Tuesday, March 1, 2011 7:00 AM

Glad to hear of Dan's improvement. Hopefully he'll be able to sing a few bars of some good old Irish songs by St. Patrick's Day.
Kathy Hiber

Tuesday, March 1, 2011 9:07 AM

Good news! Until then, Happy St. Patrick's Day.
John Ahern

Tuesday, March 1, 2011 9:49 AM

All right—great news. Thanks for the update. We'll keep praying and maybe come up to see you this summer.
Charlie Eldredge

Tuesday, March 1, 2011 12:22 PM

A third Ahern "voice" heard from—Glad you are feeling better. Until we hear from you again, Happy St. Patrick's Day!
Ellen Giles

Tuesday, March 1, 2011 7:58 PM

WAY TO GO DAN. KEEP UP THE GREAT FIGHT AND IMPROVE-MENT. YOUR NAME AND CONDITION IS ALWAYS BROUGHT UP AT OUR CLASS LUNCHES. ST. JOHN BAPTIST DE LA SALLE—PRAY FOR US AND ESPECIALLY YOU!!! BOB MC 53
BOB MC ELROY

Monday, March 14, 2011 4:32 PM

Hi, Dan—Ditto McElroy's prayer. How intriguing that March 25, the Feast of the Annunciation, commemorates the greatest news ever heard. We all look forward to hearing of your good news, too. Keep up the good recovery.

Charlie Eldredge — '53

Monday, March 14, 2011 4:34 PM

Always good to get encouraging news. Hope all goes well for you. Best regards, Bill Gerstner, HSV AR.

Monday, March 14, 2011 4:54 PM

Thanks for the update. Happy St. Paddy's day!
John Ahern

Tuesday, March 15, 2011 8:46 AM

Dan and Karen:
Praise the Lord! We are so glad that Dan is doing so well. What a joy it must be after all you've gone through, Dan. It indeed sounds hopeful. Gale and I are in Florida for about 2 more weeks. Our grandkids will be here soon and we can't wait to see them. It's been a month now since we left home. Even though snow is still on the ground at the lake, you will surely love being home, both of you. Halleluia!

Love to you both, Julie and Gale Mellum

Friday, March 18, 2011 1:35 PM

Dan:
Your handling of a challenging situation continues to be amazing and inspiring to those of us who have not been put to the test. Good you are to get home on April 9, it must be almost time for those storm covers to come off the windows and a real "memory time". Karen and I should be back from Texas by mid May and will look you up then.

Dave & Karen Michaud

Friday, March 25, 2011 9:14 AM

Prayers surround Dan and you today as he has his scan. Trusting that results will be good. One of my faith stories.... My holiday cactus is getting more buds on it everyday. Susie split my mom's original holiday cactus so we all could have a plant. Believe it or not, mine frequently gets buds and blooms many years around my dad's October birthday and/or my mom's March birthday. I hadn't seen a bud in over a year until I noticed buds last Sunday on what would have been mom's birthday. When I see those buds, my faith leads me to remember good things about my parents as well as to believe God is helping to heal and make things right in family and friends' worlds. This year I felt it was a sign that the newborn twins were growing, a friend would begin to deal with the recent loss of her husband, and I was on the mend. Now ... I pass it on to you that Dan will receive good news today! Some may call this a crazy story ... I believe God comes to us in small meaningful ways if one takes the time to look, listen, and wait. Perhaps this is how He brings me reassurance and the ability to trust.

Whatever... I pray one of those buds is for Dan today. I know mom and dad would want to share them with the Peterson family.

Take care. Karen Daniels

Friday, March 25, 2011 10:16 AM

We will be praying. Bad news for the Supervisor that works for me, her mom just received diagnosis of pancreatic cancer that has gone to her bowel, stomach, and liver. Cancer SUCKS! Love you both! Dan Collins

Friday, March 25, 2011 11:27 AM

We are still in St George, UT. Mike and Amanda are here visiting us this week We will say extra prayers for Dan today.

Bev Lindsey

Friday, March 25, 2011 5:53 PM

Dan and Karen:

If anyone deserves recovery from cancer, it is you, Dan! This is fabulous news. We are so happy. Enjoy the lake this weekend.
Julie and Gale Mellum

Friday, March 25, 2011 6:32 PM

Such wonderful news. We are so happy for you.
Carol and Lloyd Dellise

Friday, March 25, 2011 6:49 PM

What wonderful news! You must be on top of the world! We look forward to seeing you when we get back to Iron River.
Love, Julie & Jerry Peck

Friday, March 25, 2011 7:37 PM

Awesome, awesome news!!!!!!! We are so happy, happy, happy for you both!!!!! Nothing but well wishes to you Dan and I can just imagine Karen with the hugest smile right now.
Brian & Sharon Farnady

Friday, March 25, 2011 7:41 PM

How cool is that? Praise the Lord! Charlie Eldredge

Friday, March 25, 2011 8:27 PM

DAN, KEEP UP THE GREAT BATTLE. YOU ARE ONE TOUGH -SON-OF-GUN. WAY TO GO!!
BOB MC ELROY "53"

Friday, March 25, 2011 10:00 PM

Hallelujah! Prayers are answered, Dan. There surely have been a multitude of them on your behalf. This news is great. You have a new lease on life—one you richly deserve. God bless, John and Jeanne Joseph

Friday, March 25, 2011 11:09 PM

My heart is singing and thanking God for this wonderful news!!! I chose this color in honor of the Blessed Virgin Mary on this the feast of the Annunciation. I prayed for you at mass today and well as many other times during the day. This all seems so miraculous. The original ominous diagnosis was so sad. I think part of God's plan in all of this was to bring you two to Duluth so we could become even closer and my kids who visited you and your kids could get to know each other better. I love you both.

Peg Likar

Saturday, March 26, 2011 9:19 AM

Dear Dan and Karen:
It was great to check our e-mail this morning and receive this wonderful news about Dan's CT scan results. We are very happy for you Dan and for your entire family. We will continue our prayers since they seem to be working well. We will return home in early May and hope to see you then.

Best Regards, John and Pat Hancock

Saturday, March 26, 2011 9:53 AM

Good Morning, Dan and Karen:
How wonderful it was to read your great news! We are so happy for you. Now you can enjoy moving back to the lake and taking in the warmth and beauty of spring - if it ever gets here! We so enjoyed having lunch with you last week and will do it again soon. The Lord has truly blessed you - what a gift! Take care and talk to you soon.

Love, Sue and John McLennan

Saturday, March 26, 2011 11:42 AM

Great news!! Celebrate in Iron River. John Ahern

Wednesday, March 30, 2011 8:07 PM

Tough people almost always seem to find a way to get by tough problems! Seems as tho Dan and Karen are tough enough to get past the major problems that life sometimes throws at us. Thank God for the advances in the treatment of Cancer. Best of luck and the continued support of your friends and God as you continue your fight.

LeRoy Hanson

Saturday, April 9, 2011 7:41 AM

Dan and Karen, what a heartwarming message to wake up to this morning. I can just feel your joy in being home at the lake with such an ordeal behind you all. This is truly miraculous, so praise the Lord! Hope to see you soon now that summer is just around the corner.

Julie and Gale Mellum

Saturday, April 9, 2011 8:47 AM

What great news to hear that you are back home on Buskey Bay! Can just picture you sitting on the deck looking out at the lake with smiles on your faces. The long winter is over and you endured it with such courage and faith. Thanks for allowing us to travel through it with you. You were amazing inspirations to everyone. Enjoy each day as you welcome spring and summer with renewed spirits. Hope to see you sometime this summer.

Karen and Rod Daniels

Saturday, April 9, 2011 8:53 AM

Great news Dan ... I will pass it on to those who do not get CaringBridge postings ... Hope you'll be able to join your brethren for lunch one of these days ...

Mike Heffron

Saturday, April 9, 2011 10:48 AM

Hip, Hip, Hooray!!! Will be seeing you in church after a couple more weeks when we get back home. Thank God for helping you thru the winter. See you soon.

Ann Prell

Saturday, April 9, 2011 11:22 AM

Have been following the progress with amazement. Congratulations for winning this fight, and best wishes for a continuing recovery. Wishing you all our best.

Vicki and Dan Knapp

Saturday, April 9, 2011 11:49 AM

Great news Dan.! Keep up the good work and may God continue to bless you and your family.

Jay Brooks

Saturday, April 9, 2011 12:55 PM

Good! Enjoy your home and family. John Ahern

Saturday, April 9, 2011 1:33 PM

Glad to hear the good news. I know you'll enjoy being back in Iron River.

Ellen Giles

Saturday, April 9, 2011 7:30 PM

So happy to hear that your back in your own place, we know how good that feels after being gone along time. We are so happy that Dan is feeling wonderful and can be about at home. Brian & I will be seeing you the first two weeks of June, as we will be coming with some of our family.. Take care Love,

Brian & Sharon Farnady

Saturday, April 9, 2011 10:04 PM

Dan—What good news, Nice going to you and the whole family — and the docs and God. I don't think I have your personal email address. It would be good to keep in touch.

Charlie Eldredge

Saturday, April 9, 2011 10:38 PM

Didn't it feel good to say, "This will be our last post?" Praise God in His goodness and glory in providing you a   perfect day to get HOME.

Peg Likar

Sunday, April 10, 2011 12:57 PM

Hi Dan & Karen:
So glad to hear you are back in Iron River! That is wonderful! I am hoping to get out there is summer and look forward to seeing you then. Hugs to you all.

Jennifer, Mike & Caleigh (Farnady) Nystrom

Tuesday, April 12, 2011 3:30 PM

We're glad you're back home and doing better. Hope to see you soon!

Ellen Hoeltgen

Saturday, April 16, 2011 3:19 PM

Dan and Karen:
What great news to hear Dan's cancer is in remission and that you are able to go back to your home. Now if we can get some nice warm weather for his walks and just to have the sunshine come through the windows. It's time to start Holy Week and many times I think the weather is also in mourning! You are in my thoughts and prayers. I hope this is a very good week for all of you and wishing you all a very Happy Easter!

Clara Timmerman

Monday, May 23, 2011 2:46 PM

Good to hear how you are doing. I hope you are able to get out in the yard during this summer.

Take care,
Dick DelMedico

Monday, May 23, 2011 3:08 PM

Dan and Karen, I am saddened to hear about the lung nodules, just when things seemed so much better. I feel I must comment that most hand sanitizers are scented and contain carcinogenic compounds in their fragrance chemicals. Not to sound like I know it all, but it is discouraging that even doctors don't seem to know that hand sanitizers kill the good germs as well as the bad, in addition to containing harmful fragrance toxins. I think you deserve to know this, and can of course, decide what to do about it. A carbon-filtered facemask is the best way to avoid wood smoke and fragrances which inflame mucous membranes like throat and lungs. We are looking forward to coming to the lake soon and hope to see you soon. God bless you both,
Julie and Gale Mellum

Monday, May 23, 2011 4:01 PM

So sorry to hear of these continued problems. We plan to come to the lake this week, and we'll definitely call you. Hang in there!!!
Tom and Ellen Hoeltgen

Wednesday, July 13, 2011 10:29 PM

Dan and Karen:
I'm so sorry not to hear better news from you. Our thoughts are with you all.
Mary Shreves (Alaska)

Wednesday, July 13, 2011 10:46 PM

Dear Dan and Karen:
I am sorry to get the news of Dan's health. My prayers are with you.
Ellen Giles

Thursday, July 14, 2011 12:33 AM

Dear Dan and Karen:
The news from Dan's appointment Wednesday isn't what you or

any of us want to hear. The journey is taking twists and turns, going places that you don't care to be. And yet, you know that God is there with you and will continue to be. He won't leave Dan. In His own way, He will take care of him. He has already given Dan the gift of you, Karen. What a blessing you are to him. Together, the two of you are such strong people of faith.

Sending prayers to both of you for peace and understanding now and in the days ahead. We walk this journey with you, too.

Karen & Rod Daniels

Thursday, July 14, 2011 7:33 AM

So very sorry to hear about your Dr. appointment yesterday. Know that our prayers are with you. If we can be of any help please let us know.

God Bless - Jerry and Judy Darwin

Thursday, July 14, 2011 10:55 AM

It is good to have an update. We are getting into the swing of summer. I trust you're able to get out and enjoy this nice weather. I still go down to the Bank everyday. I get my mail. I really don't do anything. I have a traveling companion and we are able to golf together. Hang in there trooper. talk at you later.

Dick DelMedico

Thursday, July 14, 2011 1:44 PM

Dan and Karen:

We so enjoyed our visit with you last weekend. You are such dear friends, and it felt so good to have such nice "quiet time" with you in the beauty of the lake views and smell of Linden Trees (?) somewhere. Gale and I are so saddened to know that you are beginning hospice, Dan. You are a wonderful and brave man, and have been so every step of the way. Both of you guys are troopers and have had the best attitude throughout this "journey", as they say. We pray that God will help you be as comfortable as possible from now on. We will think of you every time we use the clothes chute at the lake and whenever we have a singing get together at the piano, Or at many other times when we remember your sterling friendship. We also hope to see you again if you're up for visitors. We're about to start vacation at the lake this coming Monday through all of July.

With love, Julie and Gale Mellum

Thursday, July 14, 2011 9:39 PM

Dear Dan and Karen:

Pat and I are praying for you. You have both been an inspiration to us from Dan's diagnosis through his extended treatment period. Dan fought, and is continuing to fight, a brave and valiant battle with a horrible intruder. We know that you will place your trust in the Lord as you move forward in this difficult time. Please let us know if there is anything we can do to assist you in any way.

John & Pat Hancock

Friday, July 15, 2011 11:13 AM

Thanks for the updates. Wishing you comfort and improvement.
Bill and Pat Gerstner

Saturday, July 16, 2011 7:25 PM

Dear Dan & Karen:

Jim & I want you to know how much we care, and please let us know if we can be of any help to you. Call any time! May God's tender loving care embrace you.

Jim & Judy Nelson

Sunday, July 17, 2011 9:01 PM

Dan:

My prayers are with you and your family during these trying days.

Bill Rogers

Monday, July 18, 2011 9:57 AM

Will keep praying that God keeps giving all of you the strength to help you thru the next phase whatever that will bring.

Howard and Ann Prell

Friday, July 22, 2011 8:09 AM

Thoughts and prayers to you in your journey now. Enjoy the time as well as you can! It's a battle and if attitude could beat it, you would win. Take care!! God Bless you and your family.
Sheila & JT Wilcox

Friday, July 22, 2011 8:22 AM

Dan and Karen:
Thanks for the updates on Dan's condition. What a wonderful thing this website has been. We've missed seeing you, but Tom as at their cabin right now, and he'll be stopping by. We'll also be there in 2 weeks with Debby. It sounds as if things are under good control and Dan is feeling somewhat better. We pray for continued good days and know that many, many people share these wishes for you.
Tom and Ellen Hoeltgen

Friday, July 22, 2011 8:35 AM

Thanks Karen for the update. Even tho I don't write on this very often both of you are in my thoughts and prayers very frequently. May God continue to be your source of strength. Ann Prell

Friday, July 22, 2011 8:53 AM

Dear Dan and Karen:
Once again your words reveal what great people of faith you are. This site comes alive with inspiration every time you share Dan's journey. Amidst all that you are going through, your words reveal how walking with God brings hope and peace to each day. He is not only walking with you; he is shining through you!

So glad that you are surrounded by caring and competent hospice people. Prayers, that both of you will find continued strength and a bit of joy in each day.

We walk with you from a distance, dear friend.
Karen & Rod Daniels

Friday, July 22, 2011 9:44 AM

Dan and Karen, I read your latest entry with joy that you are feeling better, Dan—-and that you have such a wonderful "support team" in the way of medical care, plus all sorts of friends. Please count us among them! We know this weekend is the Blueberry Festival and you class reunion, Karen, and you are busy. But are you going to be around tonight? Mickey, Sue and John, Tom Hoeltgen (here alone) and we just decided to go to meet at Hydes for dinner at 5:30. It would be wonderful if you were able to join us. Otherwise, sometime we would all love to stop by your deck briefly and say hello. We understand that this weekend may be impossible, but we at least had to ask.

Julie Mellum

Friday, July 22, 2011 10:55 AM

Your friends and classmates met for lunch last Monday ... 13 in all including Schumacher who is an infrequent visitor ... Dolan was there ... Doc is suffering from macular degeneration which bears on his golf game ... Ed Mansur was back from the lake ... Scott was there, talkative as always and looking better all the time ... All wanted you to know they are thinking of you and saying their prayers for your quick recovery ... Love and kisses...

Mike Heffron

Friday, July 22, 2011 1:37 PM

Glad to hear that you are feeling better. We think of you often and want you to know you are not forgotten even though you are far away.

Clyde and Mariam Snider

Friday, July 22, 2011 1:38 PM

I sort of feel like a ghost from the past but it's been many years since I have seen you or talked to you. Mike does such a wonderful job in keeping all of us 53'ers informed. I'm sorry to hear of the battle you are fighting but it is so encouraging to see such a strong attitude and deep faith that you and your family are showing. What a great role model for all of us.

You can be assured that we are adding you to our prayer list!
John Bins

Friday, July 22, 2011 3:01 PM

Dan, it's been a long time since talking together. I was saddened to learn of your illness. Evie and I will keep you in our prayers. Keep the faith and best wishes.
Jim Albrecht

Friday, July 22, 2011 5:09 PM

Dan, Heard from Mike you're in the hospital. Add another class mate to the prayer list.
Jerry Haag

Friday, July 22, 2011 7:34 PM

Dan:
As in the past, our daily prayers continue to focus on your recovery and the strength to endure any setbacks along the way Karen, Your courage and upbeat attitude is an inspiration to all of us. Hopefully our prayers will continue to support you as well.
Bev Lindsey

Friday, July 22, 2011 11:04 PM

Dan: Keep up the good fight, Our prayers are with you.
Jay Brooks

Saturday, July 23, 2011 2:00 AM

Mr. & Mrs. Collins:
I grew up in CG and was a friend of Pat's. I have been following this challenging journey you have been on and keeping you and your family in thought and prayer.

I'm writing to put my two cents in about hospice. I was a hospice volunteer for 8 years and that experience caused me to return to school to become a social worker. I agree with your hospice nurse that you have not signed on too soon. I am such a HUGE advocate of hospice and its philosophy. I am confident each and every hospice team member's name will end up on your list of "angels" as you will find that they will support you wholly and in more ways than you might be able to imagine right now.

I send my blessings as you all continue to navigate this last chapter of Dan's life. May it be a comfortable, peace- and love-filled time for all of you!

I will continue to be here following your journey and sending my quiet support throughout!

Lori Campbell

Thursday, July 28, 2011 5:35 PM

Uncle Dan & Aunt Karen:

Following your journey—just wanted you to know that we (and our church family) continue to pray for your comfort and healing! Glad you are feeling a little better. I wish we were closer to be of assistance—but we will be on our knees petitioning our GR8 God to perform a miracle!

With Love The Johnsons

Dan, Roxanne & Gaby-Roxanne Johnson (Peterson)

Friday, August 5, 2011 10:11 AM

Hi, Dan & Karen:

The regular updates are very encouraging and show your faith in getting back to full health. I wish I could be a visitor right now but, as I mentioned on the phone, I am looking forward to seeing you next year.

Just the thought of the raspberries made my mouth water. I never could figure out how one can resist eating them off the vine, and always wonder how so many actually make it home to be made into jams and pies!

You continue to be in my thoughts and prayers.

Love, Joe Di Cola

Friday, August 5, 2011 11:20 AM

Dan and Karen:

So good to see that your pain medication is helping, Dan. Everyone wants to keep you feelin' "frisky" for as long as possible. Not that any of it is fun, of course. What a wonderful tribute to you that friends back from high school are even coming north to mix it up with you, in addition to your other wonderful friends and family. Did you know that Debby Hoeltgen is up? Haven't seen her yet, but hope to. Our thoughts and prayers are with you.

Julie and Gale Mellum

Monday, August 15, 2011 9:48 AM

Dan and Karen:

So good to hear that you are feeling a little better, Dan. You have so graciously accepted your situation and we so admire you for it. It is wonderful to hear how good everyone has been to you in IR, including your old high school friends and great family. We too are thinking of you and with you a good week ahead.

Love, Julie and Gale Mellum

Monday, August 15, 2011 4:58 PM

Dear Dan & Karen:

It is always great news to get the good news you sent today. I am glad you are staying home this winter since it is always better to be in ones own surroundings during the time when the snow can get soooo deep.

I am glad, Dan, that your appetite has improved and that there is taste to the food. Know, as always, that there are a lot of prayers and words of love—not only from me—but from sooo many people and that this is going to stay with you throughout your journey to full health.

Mentioning snow removal, Karen, you have reminded me that I am returning to winter when I move to Ohio—-brrrrr! But, after those 28 years in FAR-GOne winter holds no terrors for me. God bless you every day.

Love, Joe Di Cola

Monday, August 15, 2011 7:32 PM

Hi, Dan and Karen:

It's good to hear things are still stable. We certainly enjoyed our visit with you both and appreciate your hospitality—and strawberry shortcake. Our trip from Iron River to Duluth was much less adventurous than our trip to I.R., and we had a great get-together with my two cousins.

We've had almost steady company here, but it looks like it will let up next week. Now that we've discovered the overland route to your home, we'll certainly try to get back there when we can. Drop a line if you need anything or would enjoy some more chat—although it sounds like lack of visitors is not a problem. Know you're both in our prayers. Keep up the good fight.

Regards—Charlie and Marion Eldredge

Tuesday, August 23, 2011 4:23 PM

Dear Dan & Karen:

It is great to hear that things are going well and, from the comments of others that you mentioned, you are looking well, too.

Wow! 50 years—I am glad you included the photo from that September 9 50 years ago. What a handsome couple—still are! You continue to be in my thoughts and prayers.

Love, Joe Di Cola

Tuesday, August 23, 2011 8:45 PM

Dan and Karen:

It was so wonderful having you join McLennans and us for dinner. I just can't believe your stamina, Dan, when food doesn't even taste all that great and you can't be feeling too hot. You are truly amazing. We look forward to seeing you at church on September 10th to celebrate your anniversary and join in singing "For the Beauty of the Earth" with Sue accompanying the choir and congregation. We hope you will have as many good days as you can between now and then.

Love, Julie and Gale Mellum

Thursday, September 8, 2011 9:43 AM

Dear Karen and Dan:

Your weekend sounds wonderfully exciting with the gathering of so many family and friends. What a celebration it will be for you ,,, surrounded by those special people who love and support you. How fitting that you choose to have a special mass ... another of the many ways you witness your faith, courage, and love for each other. You will be in our thoughts and prayers through it all. God's blessing on your 50th Anniversary. May the day be filled with much JOY!

Karen & Rod Daniels

Thursday, September 8, 2011 12:29 PM

Hi, Dan and Karen - Hope your celebration goes wonderfully well. I was so happy to see your wedding picture, especially to see our Aunt Viv and Uncle Dan.

Dan, I'm pretty sure I was in 7th grade when I was writing to you in Germany where you were stationed with the K-9 Corps. Where did the years go? What's that Maurice Chevalier song? Ah, I remember it well.

Kathy Hiber

Friday, September 9, 2011 8:48 AM

Congratulations to both of you! Pat & I will celebrate our 50th two weeks from now ... Hope yours is as happy as our has been ...

Mike Heffron

Friday, September 9, 2011 9:51 AM

Congratulations to a wonderful couple!! It's always interesting to hear how couples met— thanks for sharing Karen.

Ann Prell

Friday, September 9, 2011 2:02 PM

The Lord has walked with you for 50 years...and will stay beside you for the rest of your days. May God continue to support you in faith, hope and love.

John and Jeanne Joseph

Friday, September 9, 2011 3:53 PM

Dear Dan and Karen:
Congratulations on your 50th anniversary!!! Wish we could all be together again as we did in the past. We have a little over a month until ours. Our thoughts and prayers are with you today. Hope you have a good weekend.
Jim and Charlotte Selgeby

Sunday, September 11, 2011 7:38 PM

WOW Karen, are you quick to get these wonderful photos in your site!!! Of course you are computer literate while I am not. I have to have Misty help me get my pics on the computer. Am so glad you had such a nice weekend of celebration with family friends and parish members. Again congratulations and prayers for many more happy times.
Ann Prell

Monday, September 12, 2011 7:13 PM

Joe and I had a great time this weekend! You are an inspiration to not only us, but all of those around you! Joe and I will celebrate 25 years of marriage next July... and we hope God gives us the gift of 25 more, like he has to you two! Blessings to both of you, our parents, and we wish you many days, months, and years of happiness to come.
Love to both of you! Colleen Collins

Tuesday, September 13, 2011 9:29 PM

Dan and Karen:
Gale and I had such a wonderful time at your church service and anniversary celebration. We were so moved by everything, including Joe's "Danny Boy" sung just for you and a most appreciative congregation. We really enjoyed talking with you, your friends and family. I loved reading about how you two met—the "marriage made in heaven." It is true that you are an inspiration to us all, Brandy Moderns or not!
Julie and Gale Mellum

Thursday, September 22, 2011 9:37 PM

Dan and Karen:
We so hate to hear that it's tougher to breathe now, Dan. But it is good to know that oxygen may be helping and that it's easy to be set up to use anywhere in your house and for short outings.

I suppose a brandy modern doesn't even sound good. At least we can joke about it. You guys are the greatest and our prayers are always with you.

Love, Julie and Gale Mellum

Friday, September 30, 2011 9:33 AM

Sorry about your current swallowing problems. Coming from a former oncology nurse, a temporary gastric feeding tube is not the worst thing in the world. It provides plenty of fluids and nutrition that is needed to maintain your strength. I'm sure your doctors will advise on what is best. I bet the fall colors are at their best right now in IR. Keep on keeping on.....

God's blessings, Tom and Ellen Hoeltgen

Friday, September 30, 2011 8:22 PM

Dan and Karen:
I hate to hear about your swallowing difficulties, Dan. You are both such troopers. We pray that this issue will improve and that you'll be able to chomp food again voraciously and with abandon. (Just joking)...I recall you said that nothing tasted really good, so that is tough too. Anyway, we are thinking of you.

Julie and Gale Mellum

Thursday, October 6, 2011 9:10 PM

Praise God once again that things are not as bad as was suspected. I love you.

Peg Likar

Wednesday, October 12, 2011 8:27 PM

I'm so happy to hear the episodes of spasm are coming less frequently with the near-complete expansion of the stent. Uncle Dan will be so happy once he gets back under your wings of skilled nursing care!

Mary Starkman

Wednesday, October 12, 2011 9:35 PM

Dan & Karen:
Your courage and fighting will arc great, hope that things get better.

LeRoy Hanson

Wednesday, October 12, 2011 9:57 PM

Dear Dan & Karen:
We continue to keep you both in our thoughts and prayers. Dan, we hope this procedure will make you more comfortable and that you are soon back home. If I haven't said it before, you are both such an inspiration to us. Please let us know if there is anything we can do to be of help to you.

Love, Julie & Jerry Peck

Thursday, October 13, 2011 1:21 PM

Dear Dan & Karen:
Thank you for your update. We missed you this week at church and were thinking of you. Our hearts are filled with compassion for you and you remain in our daily prayers. God Bless.

Love, Pat & John Hancock

Thursday, October 13, 2011 11:59 PM

Dear Karen and Dan:
We are so sorry Dan has to endure more discomfort and pain. Prayers that the doctors will find a way to help the situation so he is able to return home soon. Once again, you are called to be strong and courageous. Know that all of us who care about you are with you in spirit. We hope you can feel the love and support sent your way.

Take good care. Karen and Rod Daniels

Friday, October 14, 2011 7:09 PM

Dan and Karen — It's so good to know that Dan is feeling better. Hopefully, he will be better and better. We'll keep up the prayers. Please keep up the info flow. We're with you both in spirit.

Charlie and Marion Eldredge

Saturday, October 15, 2011 11:33 PM

Dan and Karen, I'm glad to hear that Hospice is of help. My Karen can't quite grasp the situation but despite my earlier doubts about possible benefits for her I can see the diverse nature of their work, not just mind calming. I'm still using your personal doctor and thank you for him!

Dave & Karen Michaud

Tuesday, October 18, 2011 10:34 AM

GOOD MORNING!
The weather is getting colder. I still am wearing short sleeve shirts but I don't know for how much longer. I appreciate getting the updates on your condition. Wow! I say Wow! you are one tough cookie. Karen, I am still going to the Bank every day. I don't do anything. But, I get my mail and enjoy seeing what's happening. It sounds like you are getting ready for winter. I hope that will be able to get away for awhile this winter.

Talk at you later.
Dick DelMedico

Tuesday, October 18, 2011 10:46 AM

Sending prayers for a solution to the chest pain. Hoping you are able to get enough rest, Karen, too. Your days and nights are filled with caregiving. Wish I was there to relieve you for an hour or two. Ask for help from those around you when you need it; they all care about Dan and you so much and are there for you.

Take care.
Karen Daniels

Tuesday, October 18, 2011 11:27 AM

Dear Dan and Karen, We want you to know that we are praying for you and that you are in our thoughts daily as you go through this trying time. We pray for brighter days ahead and that Dan's pain can be lessened. Please call on us if we can help out in any way. We will be closing the cabin up this coming weekend but will keep in touch through Email and phone. May God give you strength and comfort in the days ahead.

Love, Sue & John McLennan

Tuesday, October 18, 2011 3:38 PM

Dan and Karen, Gale and I are praying for you too and hope that Dan can be as comfortable as possible. Gosh, it all sounds so rough. But you two are troopers like no others. May God bless you both!

Julie and Gale Mellum

Tuesday, October 18, 2011 6:41 PM

Sounds like 1 step forward and 1-2 steps back. Wish I could do more than just pray for Dan and you Karen tho I guess prayer may be the best medicine for the body and soul. So be assured that there are many prayers headed upward for you.

Ann Prell

Wednesday, October 19, 2011 8:11 AM

We hope the Dr has come up with some new ideas to allow Dan to get better rest and less pain. We will continue our daily prayers for him.

Bev Lindsey

Thursday, October 20, 2011 7:49 AM

Dan and Karen:
You continue to be in our thoughts and prayers. We hope the pain lessens, and Dan can be more comfortable. Karen, remember to take care of yourself, too.

Tom and Ellen Hoeltgen

Thursday, October 20, 2011 6:48 PM

Dad:
We Love You! If you come home this weekend I will be there to help.
Dan

Thursday, October 20, 2011 8:23 PM

Karen & Dan:
You two have been fighting an amazing battle against a giant enemy for a long time. Battles can be won and the war can be won but it is ever so tough. Keep up the fight.
LeRoy Hanson

Thursday, October 20, 2011 8:33 PM

Hugs and prayers for yet another detour in the journey. God is with you as are all of us who care for Dan and you. Take care, Karen. So sorry Dan has to endure so much pain. May the night be peaceful and tomorrow a new day.
Love you, Karen Daniels

Thursday, October 20, 2011 9:12 PM

Dear Karen and Dan:
We hope the pain is under control and you can get some rest. It takes a very strong person to endure what you have Dan, we can only hope our prayers provide some support and comfort knowing so many people care and love you.
God Bless you. John and Jeanne Joseph

Friday, October 21, 2011 7:49 PM

Dan:
We are so glad that you are home and the pain is less. Our prayers are with you and continue to be.
God's Blessings Judy Darwin

Saturday, October 22, 2011 3:18 PM

Am so glad Dan is back home to enjoy this beautiful on the lake!! I certainly agree with him that prayer is a wonderful form of medicine. So I'll continue with that medicine for all of you.
Ann Prell

Sunday, October 30, 2011 8:49 AM

Our prayers.......always....for Dan and for your family.
Ellen Hoeltgen

Sunday, October 30, 2011 10:36 AM

Dear Karen and Family, Just to let you know that we are thinking about all of you and pray that God will give you the strength to carry on.
Jim and Charlotte Selgeby

Sunday, October 30, 2011 12:31 PM

Dear Dan, Karen, and Family. All of you are in our thoughts and prayers.
Remember – "It was then that I carried you."
May you feel God's loving arms around you.
Love, Jerry and Julie Peck

Sunday, October 30, 2011 12:53 PM

Dear Karen, Dan, and Family:
These are hard days for all of you. You are people of strong faith and know that Dan is in God's care. May you find peace and strength in Him and each other. You continue in our thoughts and prayers. We wish there was more we could do.
Know that we are with you from afar.
Karen and Rod Daniels

Sunday, October 30, 2011 1:17 PM

Aunt Karen:
We are praying for God's mercy for Uncle Dan and strength for your family at such a difficult time. Our love to you all.... Caroline Walline

Sunday, October 30, 2011 1:37 PM

God's peace be with you, Dan. We often wonder, "Why me?" Especially, why me so often? A pastor friend once answered my question, telling me the Lord will never give us more than we can handle. You have been asked to handle much, Dan. And you and Karen have shown the rest of us the beauty and wonder of Christian love and living. Be strong in the Lord. Be at peace in your soul.
God bless you, John and Jeanne Joseph

Sunday, October 30, 2011 1:41 PM

I am sorry to hear that. I will pray for him to be comfortable. Kathy Hiber

Sunday, October 30, 2011 4:15 PM

prayers, prayers, prayers!! for all of you. Ann Prell

Sunday, October 30, 2011 5:23 PM

Dan and Karen:
It is so hard to hear that you are not doing well, Dan. You are such an inspiration to all of us who know you, because for one, you are such a trooper. Well, so is your whole family, which is no coincidence. Gale and I are praying that peace will be upon you all and that you can all rest "easy" as this tough time continues.
With love, Julie and Gale Mellum

Dan, Karen, and family, May you all find comfort knowing so many send heartfelt thoughts and prayers to you. What a battle Dan has fought... with a loving family beside him. Peace to all of you.
Susie and Glenn Viggiano

Sunday, October 30, 2011 8:11 PM

Praying for you everyday, I love you so much Grandpa and Grandma ~Paige Collins

Monday, October 31, 2011 9:07 PM

Aunt Karen and family:
So sorry to hear about my godfather Uncle Dan, He always reminds of grandpa Collins full of stories and full of life, except the fish story that bit grandpa' s finger. Hope the pain is down and the family is well. Thinking of you and uncle Dan and wishing well for all.
Colleen Mcniff-Mcneally

Tuesday, November 1, 2011 12:11 PM

As I learn of this I remember good times with you guys. No One could dance like you and Dan.
Larry McNeally

Wednesday, November 2, 2011 12:29 PM

It's good to hear Dan is having good days. Having family around must be especially comforting to both of you. What wonderful kids you have! How nice that you could get to Mass, too. I know how much that means to you.
God bless your days.
Prayers wrapped in hugs,
Karen Daniels

Wednesday, November 2, 2011 12:41 PM

Dan and Karen:
It is so heartening to read about the closeness of your family and how much it means to all of you. Dan, you Fox, you are such an inspiration! I hope you have a good rest of the week and beyond. God bless you all.
Julie and Gale Mellum

Wednesday, November 2, 2011 2:32 PMß

It was good to see you at church yesterday—and a surprise that Dan was able to be there. May God continue to be by your side.
ANN PRELL

Wednesday, November 2, 2011 3:32 PM

May GOD CONTINUE TO SHARE HIS BLESSINGS ON YOU.
Clyde & Mariam Snider

Tuesday, November 8, 2011 9:40 PM

Karen, I am so awed by the goodness and great attitudes in Dan and your entire family. We admire your candor as the cancer progresses and pray that the final stages will be easier on Dan. His attitude is so wonderful in trusting that God will take him when it is time and that's that. It brought tears to my eyes to see that wonderful slide show and all of you in "foxy french berets"—that was a wild occasion! At first I wasn't paying attention to the "French" party and was surprised to see Dan in a beret! I can only imagine how heartwarming it was to see the tables all set up and the hats donned. We are thinking of you every day.
Love, Julie and Gale
PS Karen, is your birthday in November too? I've forgotten.

Tuesday, November 8, 2011 10:47 PM

"Do not be afraid, I am with you
I have called you each by name
Come and follow Me
I will bring you home
I love you and you are mine."

The words of this wonderful song by David Haas came to me as I read Dan's Caring Bridge Site tonight. Karen, you and Dan are living these lyrics, you understand them, you believe them. The words say it all. May you both experience peace together during this time. We are just two of the many lifting you up in prayer tonight and in

the days ahead.
    Sending our love.
    Karen and Rod Daniels

Tuesday, November 8, 2011 11:50 PM

Uncle Dan, Jesus has prepared a place for you in paradise - may we all bow our knees and recognize His Lordship in our lives so that one day we can join together for a GREAT family reunion in Heaven! May God grant you peace and mercy - and to Him be the Glory!! With Love, Dan, Roxanne and Gaby

Wednesday, November 9, 2011 8:02 AM

Many memories. Our prayers are always with you.
    Clyde & Mariam Snider

Wednesday, November 9, 2011 8:42 AM

Dan, Karen and family:
    You are all an inspiration and in our daily prayers.
    John and Janet Ahern

Wednesday, November 9, 2011 10:30 AM

Hi Karen & Dan:
    Thanks for the update. We missed seeing you at morning mass today but remembered you had the doctor appt. yesterday. Dan, you and Karen our in our constant prayer of our hearts. You truly are an inspiration to us all.
    Our love, Pat & John Hancock

Wednesday, November 9, 2011 10:38 AM

I will continue prayers for all of you of course, but if there is anything else I can do for you, help you with, etc. please do not hesitate to call me!! I know the Lord will continue to be by your sides in the coming weeks. How wonderful to have such faith as your family has.
    Love, hugs and prayers.
    Ann Prell

Wednesday, November 9, 2011 12:50 PM

Ah, Dan and Karen. Your faith and strength humbles us. God has blessed you richly. "Yet what we suffer now is nothing compared to the glory he will give us later. For all creation is waiting patiently and hopefully for that future day when God will resurrect his children." *Romans 8:18-19*

You have borne your suffering with dignity and hope. Our prayer for you is that God's peace and promise will uphold you and carry you all of your days.

Shalom,

John & Jeanne Joseph

Wednesday, November 9, 2011 1:12 PM

Dear Dan & Karen:

My heart goes out to you that the lord gives you strength to continue through this tough time. It so reminds me of my own father's battle a few years ago. Many hugs to you!

Jennifer Nystrom (Farnady)

Wednesday, November 9, 2011 5:59 PM

Mr & Mrs Collins:

You have had a lifetime journey together and the courage, strength, and faith u have shown as u move toward the end of it is a testament to your life. Thank u for using some of that courage to invite all of us to share this time with u. The love and support u r receiving from your family and friends is also a testament to your parenting, friendship & values! You are blessed and a blessing. I am honored to have been on this journey with you... Me who knew Dan & Pat some 30 years ago. You will all b in my thoughts and prayers!

Lori Campbell

Wednesday, November 9, 2011 7:50 PM

Extra prayers and thoughts sending your way in this difficult journey. It is a very sad and sometimes lonely feeling trip, but there is truly a "light at the end of the tunnel" God Bless you Dan, and

Karen, and your great family!!! Thinking and praying for comfort and peace.

Sheila and JT Wilcox

Wednesday, November 9, 2011 7:57 PM

I love you too Uncle Dan! Caroline Walline

Wednesday, November 9, 2011 8:23 PM

Dear Dan:

I have never seen anything so neat as your letter to us all—about being ready to meet your Maker. And that even with your love of your supporting family, you can say "So be it!" That is terrific and very moving. Your attitude is an inspiration that will aid us all when our time comes. It is wild and wonderful to be able to talk so openly about end of life stuff like this. You have done it so graciously and beautifully. We all love you, Dan. You have been a wonderful friend to us all. We hope your days ahead will be easy on you and peaceful. Love,

Julie and Gale Mellum

Wednesday, November 9, 2011 9:16 PM

"Seeing death as the end of life is like seeing the horizon as the end of the ocean."

—David Searls

I love you Dad!
Mary Lou

Wednesday, November 9, 2011 10:30 PM

Dan and Karen—Our hearts are heavy as we share your journey. But we thank you both for showing us how to do "it" right. Dan couldn't have described what I assume is everyone's attitude — It's not what is coming to us all that we fear, but how it comes.

We're so glad we were welcomed to visit you last July. We'll long remember the great conversation and the delicious strawberries that Dan had helped pick.

Both of you and your family are an inspiration and a superb example of facing death in the hands of Christ. We sang the hymn "Abide With Me" at church yesterday — it's Anglican, not Catholic, but it pretty well nails the mystery of death and the hope that God's love provides.

Know you all continue in our prayers. Thanks so much for keeping us in the loop. You're not alone.

Love—Charlie and Marion Eldredge

Wednesday, November 9, 2011 10:35 PM

Dear Dan and Karen:

"Do not let your hearts be troubled. Trust in God; trust also in me. In my Father's house are many rooms; if it were not so, I would have told you. I am going there to prepare a place for you. And if I go and prepare a place for you, I will come back and take you to be with me that you also may be where I am." John 14:1-3

This is His promise and Dan, we know that you believe it with all of your being. What a witness you are to all of us! Both you and Karen. May you feel God's loving arms around you today and everyday.

God bless you.

With love and prayers, Jerry and Julie Peck

Thursday, November 10, 2011 8:47 PM

Dear Dan:

John and I were very touched by your Email. What a courageous man you are and such a shining example to all of one who has walked the journey of life with an unwavering faith in the Lord with dignity and grace.

There is a blessing in the hymnal that we use down there at St. Mike's that is of course supposed to be sung and that we used at our parish in Fargo but since we can't sing it to you I will just print it out for you as a special blessing:

May God bless and keep you, may God's face shine on you, may God be kind to you, you peace. Please know that you continue in our prayers and may God hold you in the palm of His hand.

With love, Sue and John McLennan

Friday, November 11, 2011 9:20 PM

Dear Dan & Karen:
Our thoughts and prayers are with you and the family as you make this tough yet loving journey. We think of you all often. It was about this time in 2009 when the hardest part of the journey became part of our every day life with Dad. But, your and your family are doing the right thing—you are keeping those you most love around you. We coped in much the same way.

Age is not being kind to Mom either (this is Janet writing). She became very weak and unable to walk about 3 weeks ago. Several months earlier she agreed to Hospice and they have been wonderful to her. Little over 2 weeks ago they had her move into their residence under a respite program while the hospice team, Mom, and the family decide what the next steps will be. At this point appears that she will not be able to return to independent living. Will keep you posted.

Please tell the family that Mom asks about everyone and has been following your posts regularly.
God Bless,
Bernice Philby

Monday, November 14, 2011 7:55 PM

I think of you everyday and want you to know that I love you both!
Kathy Kotoski

Sunday, November 20, 2011 4:59 PM

Our prayers for Dan and your family will continue without stopping, in this life and hereafter. Soon he will see that holy face for himself.
Cathy & Clyde Ransom

Monday, November 21, 2011 9:00 AM

Thinking of you and wishing I could be there with Joe to visit right now. Love to both of you!
Colleen Collins

Tuesday, November 22, 2011 8:18 AM

Good morning Dan and Karen:

As always we all appreciate CaringBriidge and your updates. The background on the photo is a beautiful story—thanks for sharing!

I have been doing a lot of shoveling lately and thinking and praying for Dan with each shovel full! We all take each day for granted and should make more time for our loved ones.

Our prayers will continue thru these difficult days. We are grateful for the comfort of your children and grandchildren.

Love.

Bev Lindsey

Tuesday, November 22, 2011 1:38 PM

It is with heavy heart and great grief that I received the news this morning of my dear brother's passing away. My son, Andy, and I were planning to visit him again today but it was not God's plan. I will have wait for heaven for that event. I pray that he will be greeted by my dear husband Frank and our son, Charlie. I can hardly wait for that great day when there will be no more sorrow and only greatest joy. Dan (and Karen) walked daily with our Blessed Lord on this year long journey and have been an inspiration to us all. My sympathy to all their children and grandchildren. Rest in peace, Dan. I love you all.

Peg Likar

Tuesday, November 22, 2011 1:50 PM

Karen and family:

Our condolences to your family. In following your Caringbridge site the past few months, I know how devoted you were to your husband and father. We are sorry for your loss.

Margaret Shreves

Tuesday, November 22, 2011 2:26 PM

God bless and keep all of you. Think of Dan as being there with you in spirit— smiling, young and healthy again—laughing at the funny things said and telling you his new accommodations are, "pretty good."

Love, Al and Karen Nicol

Tuesday, November 22, 2011 3:07 PM

Karen and family—May God bless him, and may Dan now bless you.

Regrettably, we won't be able to get to the funeral. I do hope someone from the Cretin Class of '53 can be there to represent all of us. We pray that our passing can be as beautiful and blessed as Dan's. Your whole family set a fine example of doing it right.

Yours in Christ—Charlie and Marion Eldredge

Tuesday, November 22, 2011 3:16 PM

Dear Karen and Family, Dan is home with our God, free from pain and suffering.

What a servant of God he was! His journey was filled with so much hope and courage for not only himself, but for you ... his devoted family. All of us who traveled with you these past months received so much from all of you. You taught us all so much about living and dying.

Prayers to all of you for continued peace and understanding now and in the days ahead. We grieve with you, but also rejoice for Dan's life. He touched so many people through his strong faith; you all did.

Blessings to you and the family, Karen.

Sending love, Karen and Rod Daniels

Tuesday, November 22, 2011 3:19 PM

Our deepest sympathy to all of you. Dan was a wonderful husband and father and we know how deeply he will be missed. He is now out of pain and is in a much better place. Our love to you all. Gods Blessings.

Judy Darwin

Tuesday, November 22, 2011 5:02 PM

Karen and family:
We are so, so saddened with the news of Dan's passing, but we know that he is in a heavenly place. We all mourn your and our loss, but are so grateful for his life. He was an inspiration to us. We'll never forget him and your devotion to each other. I wish we could be there on Friday, but we'll definitely be there in spirit and in our prayers. God bless you and your wonderful family.
Blessings from Tom and Ellen Hoeltgen

Tuesday, November 22, 2011 6:52 PM

Karen Collins and Family:
God be with you all at this hour. Our prayers are with you today as they have been in the past months and days.
Jerry Haag

Tuesday, November 22, 2011 10:18 PM

Karen and family!!! Sorry to hear your sad news!!! Thoughts and prayers to all of you!!! Remember the great times and have a great Thanksgiving!!!
Sheila & JT Wilcox

Wednesday, November 23, 2011 12:28 AM

Dear Karen, Pat, Dan, Joe and Mary Lou,
It was with sadness that we heard of Dan's passing today. Yet, if anyone were ready to meet his Lord, it was Dan! What an incredible faith he had. He was truly a servant of God.
I remember an analogy to death made by a pastor at a funeral I once attended. It gave me great comfort and I hope it will you, too. I wish I could tell the story as that pastor did but it went something like this. He said that when a man goes off on a ship across the ocean, those who love him are standing on the dock waving good-bye with tears in their eyes and a heavy heart. They don't want to see him go and the man is reluctant to leave those he loves behind, also. But when that man arrives at his destination on the other side

of the ocean there is another group of people who love him, standing on the dock and waving, ready to greet him with open arms. There is incredible joy in their hearts when they see him and the man feels surrounded by love once again. Dan has now arrived at his destination and we can be sure that those people on the other side are rejoicing when they see him!

We feel blessed to have known Dan. Little did I know that when I stopped at your house last week in an effort to be of some comfort to you, I was the one that received the real blessing. I will never forget how he stood up, as weak as he was, to say goodby to me and thank me for coming.

We will continue to keep all of you in our thoughts and prayers.

Love, Julie and Jerry Peck

Wednesday, November 23, 2011 9:25 AM

To All the Collins Family:

You are all in my thoughts and prayers. My thoughts are of a loving family, at the helm was Uncle Dan with his loving wife Aunt Karen by his side, together they raised a wonderful family. I wish over the years that we had visited more often, but the times I did see you all remains a happy memory. I have enjoyed seeing you all on Facebook and I see the "love of each others life" in all pictures posted of Dan & Karen you were both truly blessed! I know everyone of you adored your father and husband, that is a tribute to him and what a kind self less, loving man he was. I know he is at peace and shining down infinite love on you all. Take solace in that. He will be missed, but those memories he created for all of you will be with you for the rest of your lives.

Love, Sharon Farnham

Wednesday, November 23, 2011 9:44 AM

Dear Karen, Pat, Dan, Joe, & Mary Lou:

We learned of Dan's passing yesterday as we were traveling to our daughters home in Iowa. Our deepest condolences to you and your family. Dan was such an inspiration to us and our community this past year and he will be greatly missed. We are fortunate to have had the experience of knowing Dan and sharing our friendship. We will be with all of your family in spirit on Friday as you celebrate his life at the memorial Mass.

Love & Prayers.

John & Pat Hancock

Wednesday, November 23, 2011 11:38 AM

Dear Karen and Family:

Our deepest condolences to you and your family. It was our pleasure to know Dan and he was a true inspiration to many. His faith shone through even during difficult times and will always be a wonderful example. May God surround you with love and peace.

John and Jeanne Joseph

Wednesday, November 23, 2011 1:34 PM

Our condolences to the family. I was in the CRETIN class of '53 with Dan.

It is always sad with the passing of a loved one and a friend.

Sincerely,

Bill and Pat Gerstner

Thursday, November 24, 2011 12:41 PM

Dan:

I will miss you, but look forward to seeing you again in Paradise.

Love, Joe Di Cola

Saturday, November 26, 2011 12:09 PM

To Aunt Karen & My Cousins:

I'm so sorry that My Family & I was not able to attend Dan's Memorial Service. Dan lived life and faced death with tremendous zeal and absolute dignity. He has left an magnificent legacy for our family.

May God Bless & Comfort You!

Roxanne, Dan & Gaby Johnson

Saturday, November 26, 2011 12:56 PM

We shall miss you.
May GOD BE READY TO HAVE YOU WITH HIM. AMEN
Clyde & Mariam Snider

Saturday, November 26, 2011 4:18 PM

"Oh Danny boy, the pipes, the pipes are calling From glen to glen, and down the mountain side The summer's gone, and all the flowers are dying 'Tis you, 'tis you must go and I must bide. But come ye back when summer's in the meadow Or when the valley's hushed and white with snow 'Tis I'll be here in sunshine or in shadow Oh Danny boy, oh Danny boy, I love you so. And if you come, when all the flowers are dying And I am dead, as dead I well may be You'll come and find the place where I am lying And kneel and say an "Ave" there for me. And I shall hear, tho' soft you tread above me And all my dreams will warm and sweeter be If you'll not fail to tell me that you love me I'll simply sleep in peace until you come to me. I'll simply sleep in peace until you come to me."
Love you Dad!
Joe Collins

Saturday, November 26, 2011 9:13 PM

Another note from Karen on the funeral: Joe sang *Danny Boy* at the funeral. Not many dry eyes in the church during and after his beautiful song. Mary Lou and Pat did the readings and Danny did the eulogy. All four of our children made their Dad smile from heaven (and me too) as they made the funeral very special with their participation. Our three granddaughters carried the gifts to the altar and our five grandsons were pallbearers and carried their Grandpa's ashes and the US Flag to the grave where we had a Honor Guard salute with guns firing. Our grandson, Chase, played the taps on his trumpet as part of the Honor Guard ceremony. Mary Likar Starkman sang *Ave Maria* as we entered church and she sang other songs with the choir. She sings like an Angel. Thank you everyone for making this a special day for us.
Karen Collins

Monday, November 28, 2011 6:08 AM

Dear Karen & Family:
So sorry to hear of Dan's death. I was out of town and unable to attend his memorial service, but my thoughts & prayers were with all of you.
Karen Wicklund

Thursday, December 1, 2011 11:37 AM

Dear, dear Karen:
Thank you for sharing about your phone call. I have goose bumps! Yes, I would certainly say that you have received a message! There are no coincidences when you have a strong faith, as you certainly do. What reassurance you must feel. Thanks be to our loving and caring God.
Love, Julie & Jerry Peck

Thursday, December 1, 2011 1:14 PM

God is so awesome. I have a relative who died the same day as Dan. There was no funeral, no nothing. Can you imagine putting your loved one away without a good bye, without a prayer, without a thought? Dan is as close to you now Karen, as he has ever been and will always be there. Thanks be to God that Dan was able to remind you of his undying love with the song that meant so much to all of you.
You will remain also in our prayers, along with Dan.
Cathy Ransom

Thursday, December 1, 2011 2:36 PM

I am happy to hear you heard from Dan in such a special way and thank you for telling us about your messages.
Kathy Hiber

Thursday, December 1, 2011 2:57 PM

How wonderful that you received your message from Dan. One friend says every time she sees and eagle she knows her husband is watching over her. God does talk to us in mysterious ways doesn't he?

Ann Prell

Sunday, December 4, 2011 2:32 PM

Aunt Karen:

I thought of you and your family at Mass today when we sang "Each Winter as the Year Grows Older," a beautiful advent song. The third verse was especially meaningful, "Yet I believe beyond believing, that life can spring from death; that growth can flower from our grieving; that we can catch our breath and turn transfixed by faith." The season of lent is one of the church's most beautiful and meaningful seasons, yet attending Mass after you lose a person that shared your faith can be painful. I have witnessed your yearlong journey and I am the one who was blessed with your and Uncle Dan's beautiful example of how your faith, despite overwhelming grief, carried you both through such a difficult experience. I think that third verse was God speaking to me today about the lessons you taught me and many others. I love you.

Mary Starkman

To order additional copies of

DANNY BOY

or any other Savage Press book

218-391-3070

or Email:

mail@savpress.com

You may purchase copies on-line at:

www.savpress.com

where

Visa/MC/Discover/American Express/Echeck

are accepted via

PayPal

Also Available at Amazon.com